# arcadia revisited

the place of landscape

*contents*

# Preface

Vicki Berger

A map of the Great Plains in the United States tells us that bureaucrats and politicians were more influential in making state boundaries than ever topography was. On a smaller scale, on an aerial view of the land just south of Leatherhead in Surrey, we see something similar, abrupt and determined. This sudden line on the map arose from the wisdom of Surrey County Council who purchased the estate of Norbury Park in 1931 to halt the advance of residential development rapidly encroaching upon the Surrey Hills.

In June 1996 a conference titled *Arcadia Revisited: The Aesthetics of Land Management in the 21st Century* was held at the Royal Geographical Society, London. Conceived by Art Project Management as the co-ordinators of an art and landscape project for this 1,300 acre park, the conference was an attempt to bring theoretical and academic study into a visual arts programme and to consider the contribution of the artist to the management of landscape.

The lack of convergent thinking about the future of Norbury Park and the absence of an acceptable contemporary landscape aesthetic to guide it, called for the debate of the conference and the resulting papers collected here.

As the case of Norbury Park is not unique in the British Isles, the issues contemplated and explored in this publication are germane to many other sites.

When, during the 1790s, William Locke reorganised Norbury Park in the spirit of the Picturesque (guided by the ideas of one of its main advocates, William Gilpin, of whom he was patron), and invited Thomas Sandby to design a new house on the top of the hill, the manipulation of the landscape clearly expressed the cultural values of the period.

Norbury Park

At that time the function of the estate was clear. The farmland evidently had an economic role, but it also had a significant aesthetic and symbolic one, forming the backdrop to the pleasure gardens and existing as a statement of wealth. As well as providing accommodation, the house symbolised status; as did the gardens, while offering delight to the owners and their visitors. The whole estate, and often the landscape beyond, testified to the ambitions of the owner and the values of the society in which he lived. The subsequent change from the private to the public realm rendered the function of Norbury Park less clear.

Surrey County Council's purchase of the estate was a decisive and visionary act to protect and prevent the loss of open countryside, but it lacked a positive and coherent plan for its future. The subsequent sale to a private individual of the centrally sited mansion with five acres of garden severed the relationship between the house and its surrounding landscape, consequently confusing, perhaps even destroying, the *raison d'être* of the estate.

It could be argued that the function of the estate remained the same, except that as a public park its delights became available to a larger number of people than when it was in private hands. It is after all the same place. That argument would, however, deny the difference between the choices made by the wealthy individual in expressing his social and cultural status through intervention in the land, and the problems facing an ostensible democracy trying to establish how best to address the use and design of one of its most valued assets, invariably settling upon the lowest common denominator.

Norbury Park

The Norbury Park art and landscape project was, in our minds as its co-ordinators, an attempt to reintroduce an aesthetic component to all the decisions which were being made about the management and future of the park. In a place of outstanding topographical beauty, and one which had been designed in the late eighteenth century, it seemed to us inappropriate that for more than sixty years most decisions affecting the park had been made with scant regard for the visual experience of its landscape and surrounding countryside.

Landscape is rarely static and in the south east of England no longer natural. Man has intervened and must continue to do so unless we wish to allow the survival of the fittest and let bramble, bracken and squirrels take over. That is an option favoured by some ecology extremists and a useful one when there are limited resources and a lack of vision. It is, however, an inadequate stance for the custodians of a piece of land of exceptional topography in the tame Home Counties. To a certain extent, a milder approach of non-intervention has suited the managers of Norbury Park until quite recently.

The moral high ground currently occupied by the ecology movement is a difficult area in which to trespass. At a symposium in New York in 1988, John B. Jackson gave us a clue when he said: "I am one of those who believe that our current guilt-ridden worship of the environment is a sign of moral and cultural disarray, and I doubt if it lasts".[1] At the same time Stuart Wrede wrote: "Not only must we deal with the fundamental ecological issues, but we must find new aesthetic and symbolic forms for our faith in nature and the earth".[2]

Norbury Park is protected by many official designations whose intentions are worthy but tend towards a negative and nervous approach to its management. There is no instrument which dictates that the nobility and legibility of the essential and dramatic beauty of the land form which drew William Locke there in the first place, must be visibly retained.

NORBURY PARK.
VIEW FROM THE ROSE GARDEN.

In 1795 George Mason wrote:

"When I travel through Surrey and cast my eyes for miles together (between Leatherhead and Dorking) on hills and dales and beautiful mixture of lawn, wood, thicket and grove in the enclosure of Norbury, can I have the least hesitation in agreeing with Mr Walpole that our country is a school of landscape".[3]

Norbury Park, like many other sites in the British Isles, offers us the chance to resurrect Walpole's sentiment.

Notes

1    Jackson, John B., "The Past and Future Park", in Wrede, Stuart and William Adams, eds., *Denatured Visions: Landscape and Culture in The Twentieth Century*, New York: MOMA, 1991.

2    Wrede, Stuart "Introduction", *Denatured Visions*.

3    Mason, George, *Essay on Design in Gardening*, 1795.

# Foreword

*Richard Hoggart*

The streets of Hunslet, South Leeds, in the years before the last war were hardly rural or bucolic. The flora were at best ragged robin or bits of waste land, the fields of gross rhubarb half a mile away (which Tony Harrison later celebrated in a poem), and aspidistras in the homes; the fauna mice, spiders, sparrows, dogs and cats; the nearest air-hole a patch of tussocky grass with a tinker's dispirited pony grazing on it. The true 'country' was some miles away. A working-class area of about 30,000, it had row after row of cheap, back-to-back houses for the 'hands' and 'hinds' of heavy industry.

Those people who had a bit of backyard might keep a few pigeons. For the old men, mostly first or second generation townspeople drawn in from the countryside to the big railway-engine works, pigeons had become their one deeply cherished link with the land they had had to leave. They watched them fly out over the rooftop and waited, pipes glowing steadily, for them to glide back to the loft. A few, the link with the land rather closer and some energy still there at weekends, trudged a mile to their municipal allotments.

My grandmother, brought up in Boston Spa about ten miles out of Leeds, put out 'to service' at twelve, only just literate, had carried over many forms of knowledge from her upbringing; in knowing how to cook cheaply and well and in her range of home medicines. But I never remember her 'going for a nice walk'. Ten children had bound her to the living room and kitchen for decades; she was urbanised within her own generation; and so, all in all, were her children. It was an extraordinarily enclosed world, a grimy, city, world.

Not altogether, though. The city fathers, among the first of their kind, had bought a large estate just on the city's edge to the north; Roundhay Park, one of the earliest and finest of great nineteenth-century municipal parks. During school holidays in the early Thirties you could go there on the tram from Hunslet and back for a 'penny return'. Those old-style patriarchal councillors knew a lung was needed.

But Roundhay wasn't Norbury Park any more than Hunslet was Dorking. Middle-class families from that top end of town took their Sunday afternoon walks there; and kids from the other, south, side of the mucky river Aire larked around. It was not, in any sense, I can now recall, a rural experience (educational, perhaps, to the girls who lost their virginity under the trees each Whitsuntide); it was an urban ventilator; a big one and a pleasant one; but not country; corralled space, rather.

The escape, for those willing to seek it, lay outside. Like so many of the great Northern industrial conglomerations (especially Manchester, Sheffield, Newcastle, Nottingham), Leeds had magnificent, real, genuine country only a few miles outside its boundaries; notably ten miles from the western tram terminus. By the time I had reached my teens, in the early Thirties, I just knew that that was where one went at weekends. Like so many activities of a complex culture, that knowledge was not consciously offered to us. The grammar-school masters taught us to 'work hard and aim high'; I do not remember them suggesting we head for the Dales.

Those were the days of rambling and hiking, of the Cyclist's Touring Club and the Youth Hostels. I can smell rucksacks and saddles and carbide lamps and cheese and tomato sandwiches simply from hearing those titles. Promised a present if I pulled off a good Matriculation at sixteen, I unerringly opted for a bike, a three-speed Hudson at £4.95. Just as predictably I then joined the Salem Cycling Club attached to the enormous Methodist Chapel down the main road; but none of us went to any of its services. Nor did we wish to circle aimlessly round the streets, showing off to the girls; we knew we had to get away.

Here is where, as so often with things English, fine distinctions set in. The club was quite large and thirty or forty set off each Saturday. It did not occur to most of those who had left 'elementary' school at fourteen to join. Their pursuits were entirely urban. Except for odd ones: those not gregarious in the local ways, the autodidacts, those in whom something—a book by Arthur Mee from the Public Library, or a countrified piece in the *Yorkshire Evening News*—had touched a nerve, an unexamined sense of attraction to the countryside beyond those mean streets; and with them a few of the very respectable working-class to near lower-middle-class, typists, assistants in decent town shops, not seamstresses in Montague Burton's massive factory over in the next working-class district. And there were some grammar-school kids, scholarship boys and girls. It was an early lesson in the class-education divisions within so many elements of English life, and in particular of our ways of playing, using time off.

Yet the real puzzle remains, even to today. Why did some of us, almost as if by instinct, spend weekend after weekend in those hills and dales? I went there again recently, after a gap of several decades, right up to the wide and remote uplands. Once you are off the motor roads they are not much altered. The founding of the National Parks, praises be, has seen to that. And I mused again on the odd fact that an adolescent from those back-to-backs had become as familiar with curlews and pipits and hares and drystone walls and wild thyme as he was with corner-shops and working-men's clubs and fish-and-chip shops.

Those habits continued once we were at Leeds University. Clusters from different departments set off each weekend for the tram terminus, Otley, Ilkley, the tiny, half-hidden Washburn Valley. Just walking. A few others went climbing or pot-holing but they belonged to a different sub-culture; they did things with and to the land, for their own ends; we sort of absorbed it. I do not wish to sound vatic—

to imitate Auden, who wrote of the deep elemental impulse which drove him to gaze into deserted mine-shafts in the High Pennines. To us, those were neither mystical nor examples of what we later learned to call Industrial Archaeology; and anyway we had plenty of industrial archaeology in Hunslet.

Nor were we caught up with the Thirties 'healthy living and high thinking' which Orwell guyed so brutally—shorts, knobbly knees, folk-songs. But that was less off-putting than the noises then coming out of Germany, the Hitler Jugend, the Wanderlust songs. Some of us saw those at first hand in German Youth Hostels just before the war and did not greatly care for what we saw; too directed, too bossy, too earnest.

We did not pay much attention to the big houses and their grounds. Most of us did not hear about Capability Brown or Humphry Repton and the rest till we were at university, if then.

Yet there we were, heading for the hills and valleys. It used to be said that every English youth has something of the sea in him. Maybe, especially if he lives within the sound and smell and reasonable reach of the sea; which is not difficult anywhere in England. We certainly heard none of that call. We did have, not all that far down and no matter how smoky and smelly and sooty and constricted our daily setting, a strange, unexamined but powerful sense of the land.

And it felt oddly right if we were wet in those places; to have the rain trickling down our faces was a kind of induction. We knew exactly what Hopkins meant:

What would the world be, once bereft
Of wet and of wildness? Let them be left,
O let them be left, wildness and wet;
Long live the weeds and wilderness yet.

That must be why the word 'drizzle' seems one of the most beautiful and evocative in the language. And we sensed a sort of secret door-opening at those points where rough woodland met unkempt meadow—a sense to which, later, D.H. Lawrence and Kipling and Robert Frost gave words.

Yet it was all the time a defined world, in a deep sense a manageable world. We knew immediately what Forster meant when in *A Passage to India* he compared that bare, in the strictest sense inhuman, sub-Continental landscape with our Lake

District. The land around the Marabar Caves was not conducive to belief in a loving, reachable deity. It was arid, internally as much as externally. No secure Tennysonian prayers mounting surely to God from little village churches.

Trundling guns across the North African desert in the early Forties we sensed something of what T.E. Lawrence was drawn by. Just; but it needed a large stretching of the imagination; the desert repelled as much as it attracted. Similarly, as the plane passed over the Mid-West or the Canadian Great Prairies we were fascinated but put off. The towns down there, large or small, had an impermanent air, as though they had been plonked down from above in a Sears Roebuck DIY kit; two dimensional, little lived-in-depth, no hedgerows or muddy lanes which smelled, literally smelled, of the generations which had passed through them, lived, and died and gone to nourish the soil; T.S. Eliot heard it:

> In that open field
> If you do not come too close, if you do not come too close,
> On a summer midnight, you can hear the music
> Of the weak pipe and the little drum
> And see them dancing round the bonfire
> The association of man and woman...

Auden, again, caught the temporary air of so many of these North American inhabited spaces; but caught also the way in which the people would always put down roots; the stubbornness and the poignancy of these "Raw towns that we believe and die in". But not us; the roots always seemed to us too thin, fragile, insecure, shallow.

An even greater surprise came when we at last reached the Rockies. Monumental, yes; awe-inspiring, yes again though in a strangely unmoving way; interesting but in a manner which did not include anything about the way people humanise the land. For some people that is the attraction of huge, entirely bare mountains. Not for this kind of Englishman; more of a dislocating shock. The Rockies were, after the first day or two, boring. This was not Wordsworth's peace that is to be found among the lonely hills if you are getting away from crowded valleys. The Rockies were wonderful to look at but held no memories; they were like a striking, statuesque woman to whom nothing had happened; a sort of natural virgin or Virgin of Nature.

All the foregoing and much else was, to my great surprise, evoked by first visiting Norbury Park. It wasn't the Yorkshire Dales, but it was related to them in the sense of landscape it recalled, as nothing else had ever done over all those years. The later seminar and the essays in this book went some way to explaining why, but not far enough; they were all grappling with thoughts which I too, though more inchoately than the other authors, had had. Not one of them gave the impression that they assumed they had the issues sewn up.

I had expected in advance that to write a Foreword would be, for an outsider but an interested outsider, to gather together, even to order neatly, a range of thoughts which would reveal much coherence, in which even strikingly different approaches and points of view somehow converged like a set of often overlapping beams of light upon the subject.

A first and second reading showed that aspiration was not only impossible, except by a false and forced tying together, but also undesirable. I knew that scholars in my own field, the study of literature, were a disordered bunch. But though there are many different divisions and brigades there, all are at bottom in the same army. The contributors here are, by and large (which means that at some points they do nevertheless intersect) a band of not greatly connected mercenaries, pragmatists, prophets, even salesmen and saleswomen. There isn't much high-verbal-faluting; and the nature/nurture issue, that grumbling intellectual appendix, doesn't appear very much.

All of which goes to show, one supposes, that the problem of: 'What to do about Norbury Park?' throws into relief the different but always powerful emotional holds such a huge question has on so many people who march to different but in the end—we may hope—related drums. It is clear to a stranger that the subject, this range of related subjects, is still in its comparative infancy; but the argument is engaged; and will go on for years yet before glad confident morning shows. Which is why one of the contributors says the most important thing at this time is not to be tempted to do too much too soon. And why I found myself as I sat down to write this Foreword brooding on my own deeply urban childhood and on the almost ab-original sense-of-the-land which, as I had not guessed before, lay beneath it. If a reading of these essays prompts a similar personal reappraisal, almost awakening, in others it may prove to have been more valuable than they—and I—could have foreseen.

Not many common or commonly-agreed themes, then; but some lines which criss-cross, qualify, deny or reinforce one another.

Some authors here are centrally concerned with this century, even with today. What is or should be Norbury Park's relations not just with the lucky people who happen to live in or near the Mole Valley? To Greater London and the millions in and around it? How does it relate to their health as it is and as it might be if Norbury Park and other open spaces were made more accessible? What of those who, though they may live near, have no transport of their own and find public transport vestigial? The area is one of the most prosperous in Britain, very cosy for most people. So the number of those who live right at the bottom of the heap is, simply, shocking; more shocking than if we were looking yet again at Hunslet.

Behind all such approaches lie the suspicions of the Nimbys, of those who say in no matter how disguised and dulcet tones: "Keep off my grass". Some of those are, it must be said, small-minded and congenitally self-protective to a degree which, once again, recalls the powerfully divisive sense of class which runs through this nation like a seismic fault and fissure; even now, at the end of the second millennium.

If one wanted to sneer one would say that their archetypical figure, their standard-bearer, is the middle-aged, middle-class lady, Burberry trilby plonked firmly on her head, walking the two Labradors daily, happy to chat awhile with the blood sister she meets on the way, whilst the four dogs sniff around each other. The suburbanisation of Norbury Park encapsulated. That is a harsh image but not altogether uncharitable. As one of the authors here remarks: even if Surrey County Council (bless them) had bought the land outright and entirely off their own bat in 1930 those acres do not belong in any genuinely historic sense only to those who happen to live nearby nowadays and pay their Council tax. Norbury Park is part of the England to which we all belong and which belongs to us all; part of what Chesterton called our 'landscape of memory'. That should override class and money and the - in the long perspective—always temporary occupations and occupiers.

Yet here is another side to that bitten-in, unfriendly outlook expressed by the Nimbys. At the worst it sees all intruders as destructive yobbos with loud ghetto-blasters clutched under their arms. A caricature born of fright, of course; but at bottom it has a point. It would be false democracy, populism disguised as democracy, to throw the gates so wide open, to make access so easy, that Norbury Park especially at weekends became noisy, petrol fume haunted, litter-strewn by crowds. In the name of today's simulacrum of democracy, as always, that would ignore the other two democracies we should honour: that of the dead who have passed on such wonderful places to us; and that of the generations-to-be whom we would have deprived of part of their best heritage. The world is now full of over-crowded tourist Honey-pots, whose existence leaves quieter places even quieter; until the travel promoters move in as the nearest Honey-pot overflows; one more instance of how contemporary culture, being valueless, in the end sees everything, even the most intangible good, as a form of commodity. As one author here rightly says: in the dispute between the needs of conservation, especially the more fragile parts of our heritage, and the insistent demands for mass access (in the name of 'democracy' yet again), then conservation might always win. An unpalatable truth.

Which brings us to the eighteenth century and the great houses and parks of which Norbury Park is only one but in its way a special instance. If one had to choose between a theme parked Norbury Park (not likely unless Surrey County Council were taken over by the Populists—if it ever were there would be plenty of bidders, developers, exploiters); given the choice between that and a view quite rigidly true to its high eighteenth-century life, the second must win and the gates clang shut. Not out of Nimbyism nor reactionary historicism but because some things are worth preserving at almost any cost against thoughtless 'progressivism'.

Behind yet again, and it surfaces in more than one of these essays, is the entirely justified fear of the theme park approach. The theme park is the European, not only the British, version of Disneyland. But worse. Disneyland does not pretend to be what it isn't—a shameless pretence, a rip-roaring sequence of fakes. English theme parks are neither one thing nor the other. The heart sinks at the bowdlerised 'Heritage', the corner-cutting tattiness of all kinds, from fast-foods to shabby loos to plasticated 'events'. Smears across what was once landscape.

But those are not the only choices before us. Neither theme parks nor a frozen landed gentry frieze. The order at Norbury Park two centuries ago was admirable and should neither be forgotten nor damaged; it should be honoured and so far as possible kept. Yet, again as more than one author here is at pains to assert, Norbury Park has had successive and overlapping lives and they can all still be 'read off' in the hills and valleys and flora and fauna of these thirteen hundred acres. All periods have their claims and all periods are to some extent still alive there.

Against all this historic, this human and philosophical background of thought when one is considering Norbury Park, its past and its future, one partial and at first puzzling omission or radical emphasis in these papers becomes more explicable. The preparatory papers give an important place, for some the key place, to the development of Art in the Landscape. Good: and inevitably the example of Grizedale Forest is cited more than once. But in this volume comparatively little is said on that theme; it has receded to the background, though perhaps only temporarily. Why was this? Walking into the conference, having recently read the preparatory papers, one would have expected more.

My guess, and it can be no more than a guess, is that even those who came ready to make a strong case there and then for Art in the Landscape, had decided to step back for a while and reconsider its place in the light of all they had seen and heard. That would certainly have been my instinct. For the massive and complex impact of Norbury Park itself, and of the differing approaches put forward, all trying to grasp the enormity of the problems and the challenges it raises almost comically brought to mind that old joke about how one begins to describe in all its aspects an elephant. The Frenchman, the Englishman, the German and the American, it will be remembered all came in on the animal from different angles; in some ways all were right; in no ways was any one of them comprehensive. It may seem odd at first to call Norbury Park a kind of elephant but it bears thinking about: huge, with multiple possible uses, a work of nature, a friend of man and at all costs to be preserved.

But we had best leave that curious image; the point being made is that, in my view, those who want to speak for Art in the Landscape did right to step back a little. In the modern jargon, they had probably sensed a 'hidden agenda' or set of agendas behind all the talk and the papers. Or better and in Henry James's more poetic image: they had perhaps glimpsed 'a figure in the carpet' still half hidden but already looking meaningful and promising.

Perhaps that is why there is detectable in general, a certain  degree of delicacy, of careful stepping, between some of what was proposed at the conference and what is expressed here, in these papers now recollected in tranquillity. Perhaps that is why on more than one issue raised, there emerged now a 'Let's take it steady' caution; let's not take rash or merely fashionable steps; let's do nothing about which we are not entirely confident; if it ain't broke let's not presume to fix it (for in some very important ways Norbury Park is certainly not broke); let's try to understand better 'the genius of the place', its heart, its core. True, the implicit argument seems to continue, there are some relatively small but handy steps to be taken such as... But no one step should be irreversible. Let us not, the invisible discussion continues, fall into the shallow but obvious and bone-breaking trap of imagining that there may be some splendid, all-embracing plan which has so far eluded us—a plan which will recognise the claims of the past and the always more insistent demands of the present, a plan which fully recognises Norbury Park's several histories, which respects the continuing life of its plants and trees and creatures. That would be wonderful and we may eventually arrive there, at that quite late date fully to recognise and duly honour Norbury Park's archetypal role as a living monument to Time-and-Place-and-England. As Eliot once more reminded us, reflecting on his own form of Norbury Park, Little Gidding: "History is now and England". No wonder we were all, still tentative, absorbed.

All those involved with the Norbury Park project will no doubt be recognised and thanked elsewhere in this volume. That bears underlining. Some local authorities are not greatly inspired; their initiatives are usually more down to earth and worthy. All the more reason therefore to thank Surrey County Council and those who joined with them, for an exceptionally imaginative and indeed courageous initiative. There were so many other easier options.

I have said at some length that we could not reasonably expect well-wrapped up solutions. What we got was a splendidly stimulating exercise which will henceforth influence all who were involved. So perhaps one should best close by saying that the most impressive thing is that such a bold experiment took place at all; in times such as these, that is quite remarkable.

*Evening. The day's warmth*
*ebbs from each leaf of grass, as we cross the field*

*and find them at the border of the wood:*
*a family, perhaps; the twin young*

*rooted in their mother's*
*fixed attention,*

*the buck turning slightly, to watch*
*as we reach the trees.*

*If all they know is change, they also keep*
*the pattern of the world:*

*flickers of wind*
*and sunlight in the leaves,*

*spirals over water, gusts of scent,*
*the sudden white of fairy rings or snow.*

*Each sound is a mosaic*
*of frequencies:*

*before it cracks*
*they hear the broken twig,*

*and voices are the snagged threads in a weft*
*of song and rain.*

*Crossing their sightlines,*
*innocent as ghosts,*

*we come from nowhere, vanish into doubt;*
*reflected for a moment in their eyes*

*we know ourselves the echoes of a hunt*
*they have by heart, more real than we imagined.*

# *Roe Deer*

*Six Norbury Park Dreamings*
*John Burnside*

The most complete change an individual can effect in his environment, short of destroying it, is to change his attitude to it.[1]

# *Introduction*

*Isabel Vasseur*

Christo and Jeanne-Claude, *Surrounded Islands*

Art alone cannot transform a landscape whose primary need is for investment and repair. In an overcrowded island public open spaces will also be beleaguered by recreational, agricultural and ecological demands. The role of art and the artist must be assessed with the whole in a new aesthetic determined by history but informed by contemporary needs. Sculpture trails will not do.

Richard Long, *Dartmoor Circle*

The landscape has been apportioned little attention by today's city-centric visual arts world. The artist's understanding of rural problems is often as minimal and sentimental as that of the general public, except where he or she has made a determinedly rural excursion as an act of veneration. It is no accident that the work of Richard Long and Hamish Fulton, for example, should be realised mostly through photographic documentation of their experience. Like explorers, they scan the wilderness on our behalf. Theirs is a relationship to the landscape which expresses a romanticism as constant, if "less heroic than that of American artists" who, with their abundance of space, are moved to rearrange its parts.[2] Where Long will only shift the smallest assembly of stones and "prays the earth has a future", the American artist James Turrell has reorganised the entire cone of an extinct volcano in Roden Crater, Arizona, and Christo and Jeanne-Claude have dressed the world in square miles of drapery to profound geographical effect.[3] These works illustrate the range of responses adopted by artists in confronting the tensions between the historic perception of wilderness and contemporary reality. New devices are essential if the artist is to be effective in an ecologically conscious culture which responds only to secular images.

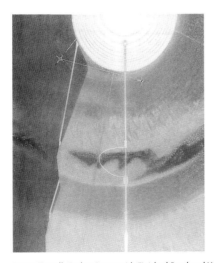

James Turrell, *Roden Crater with Finished Bowl and Western Entrance*

In Europe the metamorphosis of the artist as object maker of modern idols to one who occupies a less hermetic role has been through the historical conduit of sculpture parks. The corralling of sculpture into parks and gardens as an accompaniment to the botanical language of those places has achieved a public success which reflects as much the identity of the place as the variety and quality of the work. The Louisiana Museum in Denmark, the sculpture park of the Kröller Müller Museum in Otterlo, and Bretton Hall in Yorkshire are exceptional wooded settings which provide perfectly described areas for the contemplation of art. Grizedale Forest in the Lake District is a working forest which has imaginatively invited artists to occupy its territory as residents, duplicating the industry of the foresters to often magical effect. The wilder moorland of Inverness and Perthshire present an immaculate backdrop for the grandeur of Henry Moore, with post war works of equally monolithic ambition. These destinations are, in effect, open air galleries where harmonies of scale offer an incidence of meditation. The abundance of artists' commissions generated by the European Garden Festivals movement also realised an alternative and popular form of *plein air* gallery which did much to sweep away the elitist notion that a wider public found contemporary art incomprehensible.

Giuseppe Penone, *Otterlo Beech*

Tony Cragg, *Raleigh*

These relocations brought art a step nearer the belief of the late American artist, Scott Burton, that "Art will probably take an increasingly relative position. It will place itself not in front of but around, behind, underneath (literally) the audience—in an operational capacity". [4] Anticipating Burton's prediction, Brancusi had as early as 1935 created the famous sculptural environment in the Roumanian town of Ting-Jiu. With an axis three-quarters of a mile long and with paths and vistas which were an integral part of the work, Brancusi's park threw up a challenge which was not met by other artists until four decades later. The sculpture park, the only environmental option during the intervening period, could not hope to provide such generous interventions as Brancusi achieved in his memorial to the dead of the First World War in the comparative isolation of Eastern Europe. Perhaps only in an era which lacked the endemic cynicism of post-war Europe could the artist speak eloquently on behalf of a collective emotion, and join with society to realise the clarity of purpose required for a grand design.

Constantin Brancusi, *The Endless Column*

The present complex interplay between the artist's continuing need to reveal the world to us anew and society's continuing suspicion that the artist is at best an intermittent decorator and at worst a subversive obfuscator can lead to dramatic horrors in the name of 'public art'.[5] The courage to entertain these mistakes, however, is also a sign of a robust society which can transcend its treasured cynicism and allow artists to create new environments beyond the gallery and the museum. The American land artist Nancy Holt expresses a collective exasperation when she says "I'm tired of the isolation of aesthetics—my work has a functional aspect, like indicating sun cycles or astronomical alignment".[6] We equally respond to Robert Smithson when he proclaims that "art can become a resource that mediates between the ecologist and the industrialist".[7]

Robert Smithson, *Spiral Jetty*

Andy Goldsworthy, *Sidewinder*

The English artists David Nash, Chris Drury and Andy Goldsworthy, along with Hamish Fulton and Richard Long, have engaged an entranced audience with their rural inscriptions which seem to signal a universal desire "to repair the rift between humanity and nature".[8] Similarly the Scottish poet and artist Ian Hamilton Finlay has through his installations, gardens, and improvements, revealed an even wider spectrum of our concerns when he "uses the language of nature to dissect meaning in contemporary culture".[9] His aphorism 'in revolution politics become Nature' expresses a willingness to confront philistinism with powerful devices, texts and images made all the more effective through their placement in a gentle landscape of his own design. Such counterpoints to nature demand that he and other artists should be harkened to in the evolution of our perception of Arcadia.

The landscape has never ceased to be the material of the artist's concern: its crisis is their own and is the dynamic which has motivated the debates initiated in *Arcadia Revisited*. The generosity of imagination and the heightened observation of artists demand that they be invited to contribute not merely to the debate on the landscape, but also to those plans which will affect its guardianship and nurture. The most alert observers of visual culture can, with the craft of their eye, see better than any others what next can be done or even undone in Arcadia. My plea here is to reassert the position of the artist in the garden of the world.

Ian Hamilton-Finlay

## Notes

1   Boyle, Mark, *Control Magazine #1*, 1965.

2   From Beardsley, John, *Earthworks and Beyond*, New York: Abbeville Press, 1989, p. 41.

3   Long, Richard, *Aspects of British Art Today*, exhibition catalogue, Tokyo: Asahi Shimbun, 1982, p. 174.

4   Burton, Scott, "Situation Aesthetics: Impermanent Art and the Seventies Audience" Baltimore: Baltimore Museum of Art, 1986, p. 18.

5   A misleading, but irreplaceable term first adopted by The Arts Council of Great Britain in the 1970s to identify art outside the gallery. See Selwood, Sara *The Benefits of Public Art in Britain*, London: Policy Studies Institute, 1995, p. 32.

6   Interview with Nancy Holt by Micky Donnelly, in *Earthworks and Beyond*.

7   Beardsley, *Earthworks*, p. 23.

8   Warner, Marina, "Through the Narrow Door: Forms into Time for David Nash", *Art and Design Monograph*, London: Academy Editions, 1996, p. 23.

9   Abrioux, Yves, *Ian Hamilton Finlay: A Visual Primer*, London: Reaktion Books, 1985. Revised and expanded second edition, 1992.

# Norbury Park—
# The View Out

Gillian Darley

Painted room at Norbury Park House

In this country we are justly proud of our shared landscape of parks and open spaces brought into public ownership during this century. Yet, it seems to me, we are oddly careless about them: we use these places functionally, with much too little attention to their special qualities while those who are charged with their care remain cash-strapped and cautious. Legislation holds this public estate safe for the future, but we have not begun to think about what that future might hold.

The discussion at the symposium on Norbury Park, and expanded in this publication, offers all kinds of perceptions and insights on the public landscape, its uses and misuses. Like some smoked-over canvas high on the walls of a provincial art gallery, Norbury Park is typical of much publicly owned open space, needing a spot of attention, a wipe and a closer look.

How should we look closer? For Dame Sylvia Crowe, the distinguished landscape architect, man is "the only thinking element in the earth's ecology", but her profession which in the eighteenth century turned notions of beauty into a subtle web of psychological responses and opened up a huge moral, political and aesthetic discussion, seems to have left the stage. Increasing specialisation in training, abetted by professional polarisation, has not encouraged a thoughtful approach to landscape in recent years. There is a yawning gap, a terrible lack of intelligent discourse on the subject. If the practitioner cannot provide insights, how then can the rest of us respond fully?

In complete contrast, the educated traveller of the late eighteenth and early nineteenth centuries could not help but approach landscape at an intellectual level, in which intuition and observation were guided by that curious, yet pervasive theory, the Picturesque. At Norbury Park, the landscape did not cease at the windows of Thomas Sandby's classical house. Inside the house, George Barrett had painted a room wrapped around by a series of glowing Arcadian landscapes, each sunny vista framed by trees and trellis work. Already steeped in the Picturesque, William Locke's well-versed visitors could appreciate the scenes indoors and then press on to indulge their senses outside. They could balance the nerve-tingling thrill of suddenly revealed heights (perhaps even more unexpected in quiet Surrey, even then not a very long journey from London), set against the welcome and reassurance offered by a glimpse of the lush water meadows of the Mole Valley below. Such people knew the language of association by instinct.

Emotional charge and release, as well as the possibilities of prescribed melancholy and scenic melodrama, were arguably better provided by Georgian landscape than by even the contemporary popular theatre and its imagery. The conventions were rapidly established. When the architect John Soane went into a relentless mourning process after the death of his wife, it was to destinations such as Clifton Gorge and the Knaresborough caves that he headed, at the suggestion of those friends who knew his depressive disposition best. They had unerringly chosen sites of grandeur, natural gloom and even a certain vertiginous menace—all well established in the lexicon of emotive destinations. Soane returned refreshed and even cheered.

James Baker Pyne, *View of Avon from Durdham Down*, 1829

But equally in unremarkable scenery, the landscape architect with a compliant and wealthy client could do much to mould and tweak his material into shape— much as the dull daughter of a rich man could be transformed into a brilliant butterfly on the social stage of Bath or Harrogate by deportment lessons and some high fashion tips.

Against all this, what aesthetics are we establishing for the twenty-first-century landscape? Expertise in assessment, analysis, the recovery of historic features are in good supply. But there is little sense of modern possibility—nothing of the "acute attention to things—textures, colours, materials, forms—for their own sake, apart from the mass" which Peter Walker identifies among the most recognisable qualities of modernism in landscape architecture.

Meanwhile, we use public open space at the behest of those who administer such places (and the bye-laws which guide them). We are bombarded with fact; we can be sure of enjoying an historic deer park or an ancient coppiced woodland well informed. Armed with learning, or sometimes just with data, we stroll on through the landscape. Or we can make choices. Fishing, jogging, walking the dog, sunbathing, picnicking, bicycling... it has all been arranged—imperceptibly, but often with enormous effort—for our benefit. We are being encouraged to take a very deterministic view of the landscape of leisure.

A walk, in the English language and experience, is quite different in its connotations from the Italian or French, the *passegiata* or the *promenade*. Gently ritualised, it has no connection with real exercise or, as in its Mediterranean manifestation, with public display of the family. The British appear to walk solely to confirm their relationship with the natural world, on Sunday afternoons, on certain public holidays (Boxing Day, New Year's Day) or more regularly, despite weather conditions or season. To walk one must follow a route of someone's choosing. Within the designed landscape, this (inconspicuously) guided route can become a means of exploration, offering revelations along its way. And revelations of many kinds may emerge in the process; *solvitur ambulando*, it is solved as you walk, was the Latin epithet.[1]

The idea of interpreting a place by an identifiable route, a line which follows some logic of topography, of sensibility, even of chronology, offers many possibilities. There are examples. On a major scale, the millennial project in the landscape that has most effectively gripped the British imagination is Sustrans, a cycle route which will link the country together, end to end, a literal rendering of that rather flimsy notion, Land's End to John O'Groats. The Sustrans idea cleverly combines symbolic resonance as well as local utility, vision with function. It leads from one destination to another, but the start and finish point are self-determined.

Sally Matthews, *Cows on Sustrans Cycle Route*

On an urban, confined scale, *la Promenade plantée* du Viaduc des Arts, offers a similar route. Following the line of a disused Parisian railway running for well over a kilometre east from the Bastille Opera House, you can pick it up at will, west/east, east/west, or just for a short stretch. A leafy walk, aligned with upper windows and attic storeys, it offers variety; a small planted square below (Square Hector Malot) or a way, by steps or lifts, down to the shops beneath, whilst here and there along its length a lushly planted pergola or a raised seat provides pausing points. It offers an alternative viewpoint upon the city, and yet remains integral to it. The rehabilitated railway arches below aim to inject new life into a jaded area, whilst users of the viaduct overhead remain physically beyond and apart from the traffic and noise of the heavily used road below. Enhancing and amplifying the available perspectives on this Parisian district, the viaduct does not dictate the journey, it simply enhances the experience of walking that way.

The path in the landscape—urban or rural—is destined to be a narrative thread, the connection between spaces and events, ensuring, if appropriate, the link between beginning, middle and end. It may have no preferred direction but it has a route. Other connections can be thrown between two points; the avenue, firmly conducting the eye (and the foot), or grassy tramways, oddly virgin despite the constant traffic, linking and referring a city centre such as Basle to its suburban population in the green hills.

With different resonances, Swiss landscape architect Georges Descombes's project runs a short stretch along the edge of the wood of Lac d'Uri, between Morschach and Brunnen, well to the east of Lucerne. This is a walk designed, he says, to simply offer temptations, not to be sternly informative: "... il y a déjà trop de 'parcours fléchés'".[2] The clearing and delineating of this route is deliberately low-key, in reaction to the histrionic gestures that were threatened in the frenzy to mark the seven hundredth anniversary of the Swiss Confederation. By interposing a hint of contemporary material, inserting change of texture or subtle markers, Descombes sets a discreet signature of his thoughts and actions along the site. He acts as conductor along this seductively beautiful stretch of lakeside, offering a lookout here, a change of height there, with little more than a subtle nudge.

above. *La Voie suisse*, Georges Descombes. opposite. Viaduc des Arts, Paris

Christo and Jeanne-Claude, *Running Fence*

In a comparable, but entirely urban approach, Michel Desvignes in describing his work in Lyons refers to the possibilities offered by 'filaments' inserted through the existing fabric, to offer a crisp choice of views.[3] The itineraries of artists in the landscape, Christo and Jeanne-Claude's *Running Fence* or Richard Long's own footsteps in far corners of the world, present similar conducted tours. These are reminders of the moment against the enormity of the scene, the "intimate immensity" of Gaston Bachelard's phrase, the reduction of the general and the diffuse to the very particular and personal.[4]

below and opposite. Geoffrey Jellicoe, John F. Kennedy Memorial

Sir Geoffrey Jellicoe's profound exercise in commemoration at Runnymede offers a route with a destination, an emblematic journey in miniature. From the water-meadows of the Thames, the walk, through deliberately unkempt woods (wilderness, just glimpsed), follows a rising path of densely packed little setts. It leads on until, at a final turn in the path, there is a shift underfoot to large stone slabs with finely worked edges. Looking up and ahead, the light becomes dappled, the trees thin out and the view is suddenly closed by a massive inscribed stone slab marking the life of John F. Kennedy. Jellicoe's choice of symbolism, that of the journey of the Christian in Bunyan's *Pilgrim's Progress*, offers another level of interpretation yet the journey itself, the line on the map, then on the ground, is a revelatory gesture which every visitor can comprehend, and will not easily forget.

Memorial Garden, Montjuc

Again in a memorial garden to victims of the Spanish Civil War at Monjuic, outside Barcelona, Beth Gali's Fosser de la Pedrera represents another journey to a precise destination—this time to a place imbued with bitter memory. As the victims were once herded up to a great stone pit, now the modern visitor is guided there, by design.

Such creative tension in landscape has been all but lost in the British way of doing things. The curious visitor to the megalomaniac new French national library at Tolbiac, on the Seine in eastern Paris, mounts an exposed plinth, upon which four gigantic glass towers rear at each corner. From there, high-sided escalators suck visitors down towards the publicly accessible areas of the library. Suddenly, without any warning whatsoever, a pine wood appears below: rough, bright green turf and the scaly, elephant-wrinkled trunks of the tall trees. Here is an entirely sealed pocket park, an open space without function or entry point, providing a frisson of surprise and the pleasure of its contemplation instead.

Here wilderness has been captured, transported and imprisoned in the city. This is a botanical zoo, though with few species; an urban, heavily intellectualised comment upon the natural. It provokes, engages, frustrates, but, above all, excites. Like those heavy restraining hedges at Versailles or Sans Souci, behind which the woodland is free to get on with its growth—or is it?—a very necessary tension is established. The illusion of wilderness is often enough. Who honestly celebrates the featureless march of trackless woodland in New England, a survival of the fittest monoculture brought about by the shrugged shoulders of the suburban culture? Wilderness is welcome, within limits.

Landscape architects in the country seem to have largely avoided finding a contemporary interpretation of the *genus loci*. Torn between the impossible demands of ecological fundamentalism and historical specificity and accuracy, they retain a pragmatic view of the status quo (where assessment inevitably blocks the viewpoint of intuition) and seldom recall Richard Mabey's plea for human engagement. There is no time, little inclination, for thoughtful pause.

New French National Library, Tolbiac, Paris

We no longer need an arcane language of association such as that understood by the literate visitor to Norbury Park in the early 1800s. The notions of the sublime and the beautiful are meaningless constructs in themselves, yet their roots remain deep—touching on associational, psychological responses which we can now appreciate from other points of view. From his own perspective, Sir Geoffrey Jellicoe drew on the notions underlying Jungian analysis to reveal levels of the subconscious to which the landscape ministers. The Japanese landscape garden is layered with association and spiced with symbolism but retains its haunting quality for the unversed as for the initiate. Pastures of moss or geometries of raked gravel, inversions of scale or the captured panorama, a journey through the gardens of Kyoto is a "choreographed pilgrimage", juggling at every turn the "gorgeous and the ordinary".[5]

The thrill of sudden revelation—such as the serene view of the river valley glimpsed through a slashed window in unruly undergrowth at Norbury Park—is there for anyone, unless they be furiously pounding the paths in training for a marathon or skulking around up to no good. There is a special quality of that conjunction of scene to senses, a potent recipe for the borrowed vista which was as central to the landscape design of China, and to Japan, as in textbook examples of the Picturesque. Typically, any discussion of the contemporary landscape reverts at every turn to a series of givens; perceptual markers which no modern designer can afford to dispense with.

The important issue is how to re-establish the links between the place and the user in a way which can once again enthral—as well as simply being a useful place or 'recreational facility' in the gruesome language of public amenity-speak. After all, the dullest corner serves for many of our outdoor pursuits; it needs to be no more than flat, traffic-free and (probably) grassy. But what about delight, surprise, revelation? Let me throw the gauntlet down for the landscape designer in the twenty-first century; to combine those qualities, the gorgeous and the ordinary, with an enlightened knowledge of what has gone before and inspired by a sense of what might yet be.

Notes

1   I am grateful to Sir Peter Shepheard for this, which he believes to be from Horace.

2   "... there are already too many way-marked routes." Descombes, Georges, et al, *Voie suisse—l'itinéraire genevois. De Morschach à Brunnen*, République et Canton de Genève, 1991, p. 26.

3   Taken from a lecture by Michel Desvignes presented at the Architectural Association in London on 12 May 1997.

4   Bachelard, Gaston, *The Poetics of Space*, Boston: The Beacon Press, 1969.

5   See Moore, Charles, et al, *The Poetics of Gardens*, Cambridge Massachusetts: The MIT Press, 1988.

*In sixty years the town has come this far,*
*stopping the native hedge with pyracantha,*
*spotting the ditch with buddleia and vines,*

*but this is no real boundary, this edge*
*that wanders on the map,*
*crossing the circles of courtship and practised song:*

      *roe deer and badger; kingfisher; hunting fox;*
      *arum and cinquefoil; clutches of nettles and yarrow*
      *— all of this was here before we came,*
      *has shifted to our need, will see us out:*

*here, where the rabbit dreams, in the quiet earth,*
*out of the wind's reach, pressed to its haunted young,*
*remembering dog-tracks and snares*
*and the smell of diesel;*

　　　　　　　　*here, where the owl drifts by*
　　　　　　　　*on the evening air,*
　　　　　　　　*and the moonlight covers each verge*
　　　　　　　　*with a blanket of daisies*

# *Boundary*

Six Norbury Park Dreamings
John Burnside

# Towards an Aesthetic
# for Norbury Park

Jay Appleton

Norbury Park House, south side

Shortly after acquiring the Norbury Estate in 1774, William Locke instructed the architect Thomas Sandby to build a new mansion on a new site, and he could scarcely have made a more eloquent commentary on the ambivalence which has characterised people's attitude towards nature since civilisation began. On the one hand she was perceived in her more gentle mode as the beneficent provider of all the necessities for the maintenance of life; on the other, in her more savage mode, as an expression of danger, inducing awe, even terror.

previous page. View to Norbury Park House

In her first, more gentle mode, we can trace her back to the poets of the ancient world where you will find her in partnership with Man in the smiling cornfields of Virgil and in the well-managed, productive farms later admired by Cobbett. Moreover, while I believe the antipathy of the ancients to her more savage manifestations has sometimes been exaggerated, there can be little doubt that, aesthetically, it was throughout the greater part of human history Nature, the Mother Bountiful, who was capable of arousing the greater sense of pleasure. In her other mode she was certainly perceived as an object of interest, but not one to be approached too closely. Nobody would have seriously thought of climbing Mount Olympus to see if the gods really were cavorting about on the top of it. Mortal intruders were kept at bay not only by the fear of divine retribution, but simply by the idea of a place which seemed to fulfil a useless role in the provision of human needs. Throughout the Middle Ages a different theology (later so dramatically expressed in Holman Hunt's painting *The Scapegoat*) equated the wilderness with a Judaeo-Christian tradition of evil. Rocks and cliffs were seen as the expression of a failure of divine workmanship, that is to say a success for the Devil.

Holman Hunt, *The Scapegoat*, 1854

In England by 1700, what was most admired in the landscaping of a park was the extreme expression of order in geometrically regular shapes—a style perfected in France under the influence of André le Nôtre and, by the end of the 1600s, universally accepted as the fashionable style of the landowning aristocracy throughout Western Europe. Today, it is best seen in France in Le Nôtre's own work, for example at Vaux-le-Viscomte and Versailles, or in England in those parks and gardens which survived the so-called 'Improvers' of the eighteenth century. In the Home Counties Hampton Court and Bushey Park are perhaps as good examples as any. The symbolic message is fairly clear: living plants were important as one of the raw materials of an art form, but they had to be so arranged as to suggest an underlying order imposed by the will of man and leaving no doubt who was in control. It was not until the eighteenth century that Western European societies had generally acquired the self-confidence to seek aesthetic pleasure in nature as she appeared in her more savage moods.

above. Versailles. opposite. Claude Lorrain, *Landscape with Hagar and the Angel*.

Petworth House, West Sussex

For, by about 1730 the fashion had radically changed. All those qualities—regularity, symmetry, and the perfection of geometrical forms—were replaced by their precise opposites, as landowners and professionals combined to move in the direction of a more natural environment in which nature could be allowed, within limits, a little more freedom to express her personality.[1] But practitioners like William Kent and Capability Brown, who had spearheaded this new approach, were perceived by some as not having moved far enough and a new movement, generally known as The Picturesque, subsequently advocated a much more extreme expression of the wilder side of Nature.[2] The Grand Tour, a familiarity with the works of the Italian landscape painters of a century earlier (Nicolas Poussin, Salvator Rosa, Gaspard Dughet and, above all, Claude Lorrain), together with a new interest in the more 'picturesque' parts of Britain fostered by writers like William Gilpin (an acquaintance of Locke), led to a belief that the environs of a mansion would be more pleasing if landscaped in such a style.[3]

Beetling cliffs at Hawkstone

View from Norbury Park towards Box Hill

The problem was, however, that such a policy required no small measure of co-operation from nature herself. While Capability Brown could make you a grass sward punctuated with clumps of trees and surrounded with a belt of woodland almost anywhere, the occurrence of beetling cliffs and roaring cataracts was seriously limited. Where they did occur, chiefly on the palaeozoic and metamorphic rocks in the north and west of Britain, they rarely coincided with the parks and gardens of the aristocracy and landed gentry.[4] Although the Home Counties were relatively poorly endowed with such opportunities for creating dramatic landscapes in the approved Picturesque style, one of the few really good potential sites, as judged by these criteria, was to be found in the residual chalk plateau on the Norbury Estate.

This little plateau is, geologically speaking, a fragment of the North Downs; that outcrop of the chalk which rises from underneath the London Basin and is crossed by a series of rivers flowing northward out of the Weald; from the Wey in the west to the Canterbury Stour in the east, through gorges which they have cut through the chalk escarpment. It is one of these, the River Mole, whose valley so sharply defines the eastern limit of the Norbury Park plateau. The western limit is less clearly defined, as the ground slopes more gently towards the undulating succession of ridges and dry valleys typical of the chalk.

As it exists today the park contains the legacy of these two landscape types symbolising nature in the two modes I have described. The plateau, with its steep slopes, woodland, scrubland, and small patches of more open land, symbolically expresses the idea of that primitive, more natural environment which so excited the writers on the Picturesque. I will call it 'the Picturesque core'. The peripheral zone, what I will call 'the Farmland fringe', is, by contrast, suggestive of nature productive, fecund and conscripted in the service of our species. And although the map evidence shows that both landscapes have clearly changed since the eighteenth century, they still represent that striking contrast of symbolic types which confronted William Locke when he decided to move his residence from the site known as The Priory to the crest of the plateau.[5] I have little doubt that Capability Brown could have made an excellent job of the original site on the low-river terraces within the meander of the River Mole, but if the opportunities latent in the whole available site were to be seized the house itself had to be moved from the tame, comfortable, homely landscape type to the more 'sublime' environment of the plateau, in spite of the attendant difficulties of access, water-supply and exposure to the elements.

Farmland fringe, Norbury Park

So, what has all this to do with the future development and management of Norbury Park? The answer, I suggest, is that we have by no means worked the Picturesque out of our system.

In advocating a return to the wilder manifestations of nature, the Picturesque movement incorporated a number of ideas which have little relevance to us now, and mainly attract criticism, even ridicule, from those who are unimpressed by the antiquarian element. In architecture, for example, it revived features of medieval design like battlements and arrow-slits, long rendered functionally irrelevant. It re-introduced gothic windows and vernacular features of cottage design. It venerated rusticity to the point of infatuation and where it did not inherit *bona fide* ruins it did not hesitate to build them. All these things we should probably regard today as 'over the top'. They prompt descriptive terms like kitsch, twee, pastiche and, although certain trends in postmodernist architecture may vaguely suggest a move of fashion in that direction, I cannot see the general public, much less the gurus who influence its taste, seriously wishing to go back to this kind of thing.

But in our attitude to nature many of us would find a remarkable affinity with people like William Gilpin, Richard Payne Knight, or their successors in America who founded the Hudson River School of Painting and who eventually came to recognise the wilderness as an item of heritage very much older than the legacy of Greece and Rome.[6] Indeed, anyone contemplating the development of the Picturesque core of Norbury Park could do worse than read Uvedale Price's famous essay on the Picturesque, written in 1794.[7] It is fashionable in some quarters to denigrate styles and fashions of the past on the grounds that we should have the inventiveness to devise new landscapes for the future, unencumbered by any commitment to principles of design tailor-made for an aristocracy whose values and mores we no longer regard with favour. Those who hold this view, however, may reasonably be asked to explain why it is that hundreds of thousands of visitors every year pay good money for the privilege of enjoying these same landscapes, unless there is something about them which directly appeals to a different public of a different period and a different social class.

It is the search for this 'something' which has prompted some of us to look for linking principles which transcend the bounds of culture, place and period, and reflect more universal responses to the environment as visually perceived, not denying the cultural differences, but giving due recognition to the similarities. I must make it clear, however, that the following interpretation is a personal one and embodies an approach which still arouses antagonism among some more traditional writers and thinkers.

It is some seventy years since the American philosopher John Dewey set out a view which is now generally subsumed under the name of 'American Naturalism' and which is still regarded with suspicion in what may be considered as the mainstream of aesthetic thought. Darwinism, on which it heavily relies, similarly took several decades before it came to be regarded as scientifically orthodox so I would not immediately expect to convince everyone of the validity of my argument which is essentially an application of Dewey's thinking to the subject of landscape.[8] For our taste in landscape, I would argue, is not wholly a product of cultural influences, but these, important as they are, mould and modify a rudimentary system of instinctive responses in which behaviour conducive to survival is ensured by the operation of the pleasure principle. In Darwinian terms, environmental perception is the key to environmental information; environmental information is the key to environmental adaptation; environmental adaptation is

Benjamin Pouncy after Thomas Hearne: An "Undressed Park"

the key to the survival of the individual and ultimately of the species; and the whole sequence is put into operation because it is passionately in our nature to want to explore.

Within this system of environmental perception there emerges one area of particular importance: the awareness and understanding of any intimations of danger. To be able to deal with these we need to familiarise ourselves with the boundaries between safety and danger and we need to be impelled by our own inclinations to do just that. Facets of behaviour like seeing, hiding, sheltering, escaping and so on, are central to our strategy for survival and the recognition of opportunities to put this strategy into practice causes us pleasure.[9] So it is small wonder that what inspired William Locke two centuries ago should equally appeal to us today, and for evidence that this is so one has only to look to such phenomena as the popularity of the wilderness cult and of such activities as skiing, caving, rock-climbing, fell-walking, orienteering, or simply exploring a natural, or at least a quasi-natural environment, with or without the dog. Some fascination with what the eighteenth-century writers called 'The Sublime' is not only understandable, it is indispensable as a part of our make-up; the most important weapon in our armoury when we confront Nature, not as the Mother Bountiful, but in her more awe-inspiring mode as the tyrannical mistress.

Benjamin Pouncy after Thomas Hearne: A Park "dressed in the modern style"

Whether you accept this interpretation or not, it is an unarguable fact that all the more highly developed creatures experience a persistent attraction towards particular kinds of environment, and it is this which keeps them within the habitats proper to their species, thereby ensuring the best chances of survival. Is it really likely that such a successful mechanism should have died out only in our species? The fact that we cannot explain exactly how something works does not mean that it cannot be true and we must therefore respect the wishes of those who, from time to time, feel a need to revive what they feel to be a natural bond between themselves and a visual environment in which they feel comfortable, whatever the reason. It is because these ideas permeated the thinking of the Picturesque that I have singled it out as having more relevance to our present problems than other styles and fashions of the past. It was the Picturesque for which Norbury Park had been, as it were, prepared by nature, and it was Locke and Sandby who recognised this and seized the opportunity to exploit it when the tide of fashion turned in that direction. By reconsidering the Picturesque, we may derive some guidance for the future development and management of Norbury Park.

Walking in the park is essentially an act of exploration culminating hopefully in a process of discovery. The writers of the Picturesque understood this very well when they urged that this process should be a gradual one, so that the pleasure it affords can be prolonged and not exhausted all at once. 'Partial concealment', one of their favourite terms for example, implies an element of mystery, a quality accorded great importance in landscape aesthetics by present-day environmental psychologists.[10] Variation, contrast, and surprise are other attributes which constantly figure in the literature of the Picturesque and these can be greatly enhanced in the landscape by imaginative planting schemes and footpath layouts. Among the devices which can help to arouse continuously changing interest and surprise, deflections in pathways stimulate expectations which are not immediately satisfied. A series of such experiences can thus be strung together to create an extended venture. The secret is to find a satisfying balance between maintaining an element of mystery and disclosing the whole reality—wondering and discovering step by step.

Recognition should also be given to another frequent admonition of Uvedale Price and his fellow-thinkers, namely to leave as much to nature as possible. Whether this last principle should extend to preserving the huge dead tree trunks, which are a conspicuous feature of the Norbury Park skyline, is another matter. Those who urge this policy can claim that a natural environment should contain remnants of the whole life-cycle of the plants which make it what it is, and that dead wood, by providing a home for saprophytes, insects, etc., can contribute to the food-chain and thereby diversify the fauna and flora. Those who argue on the other side make the point that these dead trunks are overwhelmingly dominant— in short, out of scale. After all, their size is related to the height of a tree canopy which, at least in their immediate vicinity, is no longer there since their neighbouring giants have been long removed and replaced by lowlier vegetation. By now, it may seem questionable whether the arts have any place in Norbury Park at all, but if you will allow me to persist a little longer with my argument that the pleasure of environmental exploration derives ultimately from innate patterns of survival behaviour, I will go on to argue that a similar explanation underlies most of the pleasures we derive from the arts.

Consider for example a few phenomena which we regularly associate with the arts. Imitation, which is the basis of representational painting and a feature of music, ballet, and much else, is also basic to survival behaviour. It is what enables the young of all species to profit from the experience of their predecessors. Replication, the ability to produce out of physical matter objects which conform to some independent pattern, was to be found in birds' nests long before it became the objective of the sculptor. Anticipation, which in rhyming metrical verse enables us to predict how a line will end just before it does, is crucial in the game of survival. A creature which can correctly predict what is going to happen just before, rather than just after it does, has far better prospects than one which cannot. Animal experiments which test a creature's capacity to do this are designated by scientists under the heading of 'rhyme'. Analogy, the device employed to draw inferences about one experience by comparing it with another, is as fundamental in the arts as it is in the strategy of survival.

Whenever artists employ any of these devices—imitation, replication, anticipation or analogy—they are borrowing from the basic mechanisms of survival on which life itself depends, and you cannot get much more fundamental than that. Within this context it is not unreasonable to see a walk in the woods as an art form, a kind of miniature theatrical performance, a little exercise in make-believe in which we try to re-create a semblance of that primitive relationship between ourselves and the closest available representation of the natural habitat of our species. Since this requires some suspension of disbelief, any intrusion which breaks the spell is likely to be unwelcome. For most people electricity transmission lines or a large corrugated iron shed, for example, could destroy the illusion. For some people any artefact, whatever its claim to aesthetic excellence, is an unwelcome intrusion.[11]

Even if you are unconvinced by my biologically-based approach, I think you will agree that it would be fairly incongruous if, at the very moment when the philosophers are at long last bringing back nature into aesthetics, we were to forbid the arts from coming back into nature.[12] Many artists today are able to find inspiration in the built environment in which they live, without going back to look for it in the countryside; but not all of them are content to leave the exploration of our relationship with nature to the scientists who have made most of the running in recent decades. It is they who have fed the media the big environmental stories like toxic waste, nuclear fall-out, global warming, and the hole in the ozone layer. It is they, too, who have begun to advance, through genetics, ecology, ethnology, environmental psychology etc., an understanding of our own role in a 'systems' approach to the natural world, and we should not be surprised if some of our more enterprising artists should feel that the time has come for them to join in.

I am not suggesting, of course, that we should see the arts and the sciences as inevitably destined to be in competition with each other. Though their methodologies are in some ways incompatibly different, their objectives are in a broad sense the same—to explore and as far as possible explain anything which lies within the field of human experience.[13] For the scientists this involves compliance with a rigid set of rules, the breaking of any one of which would invalidate their results and not improbably destroy their findings according to the accepted principles of logic and fallacy-free rational argument. Artists, on the other hand, are entitled to range freely beyond or behind the frontiers of science without any obligation to spell out their findings in logical, rational language. The only rule they simply have to obey is never to represent the outcome of their work as if it carried scientific authority. Subject to these conditions it is not only permissible but necessary to view the arts and the sciences not as rivals, but as partners.

Most of us would not wish to be seen as standing in the way of artists if they wish to undertake new ventures in a natural world rather than a built environment, provided, we might add, it is not in our backyard. Unfortunately there are not many places in the Home Counties which are not perceived by somebody as being in their backyard! So, if we are to encourage artists to come into Norbury Park, what are we to require of them? In my view it is up to artists to come forward with innovative ideas. It is not the business of laymen to instruct them. Programmes devised and imposed by inexperienced outsiders rarely, if ever, achieve anything artistically worthwhile. But we are living in an age when practitioners in many of the arts feel that, having traditionally practised in studios, galleries, theatres, workshops, and other indoor environments, it may well be that they could develop new dimensions of their work by moving into the open air. Actors have been doing this since the time of Aeschylus and Aristophanes; sculptors for as long, if not longer. Others have invented new art forms such as *son et lumière* where a natural outdoor venue may have a crucial role to play in linking music, illumination, narrative and scenery. If artists put their case the public has a right to consider and reject it, but not to dismiss it unheard.

Gateway to Norbury Park, demolished

In a recent issue of the official organ of The Landscape Institute, the landscape architect Maggie Gilvray wrote, "As well as the management of the resource, recreation involves people—as individuals and groups—who have different aspirations and objectives. Without a consensus of sometimes conflicting interests, the project is unlikely to 'get off the drawing board'".[14] This might well be adopted as the motto for anyone embarking on the preparation of an overall plan for Norbury Park. There is a predictable reluctance on the part of the existing users of the park to envisage any change and, for the reasons I have already given, their sentiments must be respected. But if they could be assured that the central core of the park, essentially the high chalk plateau and its fringing slopes, was guaranteed to be subjected only to such modifications as were consistent with the principles of the Picturesque, which in practice would mean that its general character would be little changed, it would only be reasonable to expect them to assent, subject to proper safeguards, to the introduction of some innovations into its periphery. The periphery, of course, consists principally of what I have called 'the Farmland fringe', and it is not likely that this type of landscape would offer what artists are looking for; almost certainly they would want to be in the Picturesque core. Limited incursions into this area are more likely to be acceptable if they do not intrude on the peace and quiet of other users and if they are sited with easy, independent access from the peripheral car parks so that they can be reached with a minimal impact on the Picturesque core itself.

The opportunities at Norbury Park for visual improvement are, however, by no means confined to the Picturesque core, and some of these could be addressed in the course of general long-term maintenance. Most visitors, for example, must be struck by the poor condition of some of the fencing which in places is rusty and untidy, and will involve major expense in the long if not the medium term. A modern wire fence can be an efficient and cost-effective device for containing livestock, but it is not generally admired as an aesthetic feature of the countryside in comparison with the traditional quickset hedge, which not only has the advantage of signalling the idea of enclosure within an otherwise exposed terrain, but also greatly enhances a farmed landscape as a habitat for wildlife, providing cover, nesting-sites, and channels of communication linking places of refuge.[15]

When, therefore, the time comes to spend money on repairing or renewing wire fencing, it is reasonable to argue that serious consideration should be given to the practicality of replacing it with new hedgerows. This would be one policy likely to engender virtually no opposition since it is wholly in line with contemporary attitudes to conservation as the hedgerow has a far more respectable historical pedigree than the wire fence. Even if the costs of planting and maintenance were somewhat heavier, a determined local authority might well see itself as being in a far better position than the ordinary commercial farmer to set an example by returning the Farmland fringe to something more closely resembling the traditional appearance of the Surrey countryside.

One reason for giving due consideration to the appearance of the Farmland fringe is that it is impossible, except at the southern car park, to enter the Picturesque core from the public road without passing through it. The Picturesque core, in other words, is first perceived across a foreground, occasionally of arable, but more often of grass fields. In pictorial terms the two components are integral parts of the whole composition; the foreground is bound to influence the way we perceive the middle ground and the distance. So, if we see the landscape as a picture and analyse it in these terms, particular significance attaches, first, to the nature of the foreground, and, second, to its further margin, the interface between farmland and woodland.

Arable and grassland foregrounds can make quite different impacts on the way we perceive the whole picture. An arable field at harvest time is a potent symbol of nature the bountiful, and has often been used as such by landscape painters, but in the winter or early spring its ploughed surface has quite a different effect. When we look at any surface one of the questions we subconsciously ask is whether we could walk across it. Whether we actually want or intend to do so is not the point. At this first moment of spontaneous apprehension we are experiencing the symbolic impact of what we see, and a ploughed surface, while it may be visually interesting, is not inviting.

A grass surface on the other hand, does suggest the possibility of entering and passing across it. If the ploughland is a 'keep-out' sign the grass sward is a 'come-

Norbury Park

in' sign. We may at the same time be receiving many other messages. A bull in a grass field or even a notice threatening trespassers with prosecution may reverse the message! Even a hedgerow, which on other grounds may enhance the attraction of the field, can also contribute to the sense that it may not offer such easy passage after all. Issues of environmental aesthetics are full of apparent ambivalences and even contradictions of this sort, and, on top of that, we all read these signals in different ways, depending on the patterns of response we have developed through the sum of our individual experiences.

If there are significant differences to be observed in the surfaces which form the foreground of this typical picture of Norbury Park, the zone of contact between it and the Picturesque core is even more significant. The 'edge-of-the-wood' is as important a feature in landscape aesthetics as in ecology, where, as any zoologist will confirm, it plays a unique and highly important role.[16] In an area like southern England probably the most conspicuous contrast in landscape types is that which distinguishes between what we may call 'landscapes of exposure' and 'landscapes of enclosure or seclusion', affording respectively opportunities to see and opportunities to hide or shelter. The open farmland represents the former, the woods the latter, and the juxtaposition of the two types suggest, in pictorial as in ecological terms, the best of both worlds.

Norbury Park is already well endowed with a rich diversity of visual forms in the Picturesque core. Where there is scope for further capitalising on this is in the treatment of the interface between outside and inside. A straight edge to a wood, particularly if bounded by a fence, does not communicate the idea of an invitation to enter to the same extent as an irregular frayed edge. A famous landscape architect who was particularly sensitive to the aesthetic implications of this particular phenomenon was Humphry Repton. In her biography of Repton, Dorothy Stroud reproduces Repton's drawings from the *Red Book* of Bayham Abbey in Kent, contrasting the view as it was with what he intended it to look like.[17] The former shows a hillside of hedged fields backed by woodlands with uncompromisingly straight edges. In his proposed improvement Repton removes

the hedgerows and 'frays' the edges of the woodland, effectively breaking down the interface between 'inside' and 'outside', and I suspect that even the most enthusiastic defender of the hedgerow would agree that the proposed innovation was aesthetically an improvement.

I have little doubt that the application of this treatment to the woodland edge at Norbury Park would be generally beneficial, but this case cogently illustrates the problem that, even if we can identify solutions which are aesthetically to be preferred, we may be constrained by the practical requirements of forestry and farm management. So it may be that for purposes of stock control a fence cannot be dispensed with, and since there are problems in setting such a fence back into the wood we may have to provide some sort of impediment which will re-establish

Humphry Repton, drawing of Bayham Abbey, Kent, showing the landscape as it was

Humphry Repton, drawing of Bayham Abbey, Kent, showing the proposed improvements to the landscape

the visual interface between the wood and the grassland fringe. If so, a live hedge would certainly be better than a wire or even a timber fence, but in either case we should lose that 'come-in' invitation which is such a compelling feature of Repton's design for Bayham Abbey.

Another problem relating to the creation of a pleasing 'edge-of-the-wood' effect is that the trees here may be subject to more severe wind conditions than those growing further into the wood, and not only the choice of species but also their disposition may have to be guided by this, rather than the securing of a particular aesthetic objective. To determine how best to resolve these problems it will be necessary to be guided by the advice of specialists. No tree-planting scheme, however perfect aesthetically, will be of any use if the trees won't grow!
If, however, compromises can be achieved between what is aesthetically desirable and what is managerially possible, solutions which will work for new plantings will also very likely be applicable to established plantations. During the post-war period the Forestry Commission has seriously addressed this issue and now has a large accumulation of experience in solving the problem of making the edge-of-the-wood look more inviting.

An equally important component of the Picturesque landscape was water and I need hardly stress its ambivalent role symbolising, like Nature herself, a basic necessity for survival, but also a potential source of danger. I cannot help feeling that water at Norbury Park has not yet been fully exploited. I am not thinking so much of the big dramatic devices like fountains and cascades, but at a time when much importance is being attached to such features as wetland habitats, bog gardens, and so forth, the opportunities afforded by the River Mole for creating such facilities, if not ornamental water-wheels, fishponds, etc., might be worth further investigation. Again, however, physical constraints may have the last say. Water played a crucial role in the world of the Picturesque and its use might add in many ways to the attractiveness of the chalk plateau as at Norbury Park, but, even if it were to be pumped up from the River Mole it would soon trickle away through the permeable limestone. Any large scale use of water at Norbury Park, therefore, would in practice be geologically confined to the alluvium and river terraces of the Farmland fringe on the eastern side of the park. In any case, the notoriously erratic regime of the River Mole might prove to have the last word. At the very least it seems incongruous that the riverside footpath should apparently stop just at the point where the river enters its most picturesque section near the southern portal of the railway tunnel.

Any plans for Norbury Park, however, will inevitably be subject to a number of practical constraints. I will exemplify just three. First, on a site like this, physical geography will obviously limit the possibilities of development. We must, as Pope said, "Consult the genius of the place in all".[18] Viewpoints, for example, so important in the thinking of the Picturesque, are among Norbury Park's chief assets, but their precise locations are virtually determined by the lie of the land. Second, a major source of constraint is to be found in the concern and involvement of outside bodies. The park is in a Green Belt and an Area of Outstanding Natural Beauty. Much of it is designated as a Site of Special Scientific Interest. Contractual obligations are in place, with English Nature for example, and any further development is subject to general planning policy and procedures. All these bodies have quite specific interests in some particular aspect of the park into which aesthetic objectives have to be accommodated as best they can. Third, there are restraints of a financial and commercial kind. If you are going to feed a sawmill from the park's forest products you cannot ignore the accepted principles of commercial forestry any more than you can defy the principles of sound farm management in the Farmland fringe.

Finally, while I would certainly recommend learning from the experience of other projects elsewhere, one must counsel against the expectation of finding exactly the right models. One would not, I think, be tempted to emulate what is on offer at Polesden Lacey—Norbury Park is not that sort of park—but one might with profit borrow ideas from say, Grizedale Forest Park in the southern part of the Lake District.[19] Another sculpture trail that is frequently quoted as a possible model is that at Beechenhurst Lodge in the Forest of Dean.

But practical landscape aesthetics is essentially about people and their interaction with their environment, and if I had to conclude with a single message it would be this. School children at playtime are invariably capable of working out their own games. The role of the tactful teacher may occasionally involve intervening to break up a fight, but normally it is just to ensure that the children do not get in each other's way, as they inevitably do if everybody is allowed to do everything everywhere. In this light, thirteen hundred acres isn't a bad size for a playground!

Longleat, Wiltshire

## Notes

1. A useful and accessible summary of these changes will be found under "Garden and Landscape Design" in *The Encyclopaedia Britannica* (Macropedia), 5th Edition, Chicago: 1990, Vol. 19, pp. 655-671.

2. For example, Hussey, Christopher, *The Picturesque: Studies in a Point of View*, London: Putnam, 1927; also the periodical *The Picturesque*, 1992–Present.

3. Possibly the best place in England to find an example of this is at Hawkstone Park in Shropshire, developed during the closing decades of the eighteenth century and recently restored after a period of dereliction. See *Hawkstone: A Short History and Guide*, Hawkstone Park Leisure, 1993.

4. Appleton, Jay, "Some Thoughts on the Geology of The Picturesque", *Journal of Garden History*, Vol. 6, 1986, pp. 270-291.

5. For example, Tycho Wing's plan of 1731 in the Guildford Muniment Room, Surrey.

6. van Zandt, Roland, *The Catskill Mountain House*, New Brunswick/New Jersey: Rutgers University Press, 1966, pp. 153 and 154. Clough, Wilson O., *The Necessary Earth*, Austin: University of Texas Press, 1964, p. 5.

7. Price, Uvedale, *An Essay on the Picturesque, as compared with the Sublime and the Beautiful; and on the Use of Studying Pictures, for the Purpose of Improving Real Landscape*, London: Robson, 1794.

8. Appleton, Jay, *The Experience of Landscape*, Chichester: Wiley, 1975, revised edition 1996.

9. Appleton, Jay, *The Symbolism of Habitat, an Interpretation of Landscape in the Arts*, Seattle: University of Washington Press, 1990.

10. For example numerous publications by Stephen and Rachel Kaplan, not least *The Experience of Nature: a Psychological Perspective*, Cambridge: Cambridge University Press, 1989.

11. Appleton, Jay, "To Please or not to Please", *Landscape Design*, 194, 1990, pp. 16 and 17.

12. As late as 1968 Hepburn, Ronald, "Aesthetic Appreciation in Nature", Osborne, Harold, ed., *Aesthetics in the Modern World*, London: Thames and Hudson, was complaining that contemporary writings on aesthetics attended almost "exclusively to the arts and very rarely to natural beauty", (p. 59). A decade later philosophers like Mary Rose ("Nature as an Aesthetic Object", *British Journal of Aesthetics*, 16, 1976) and Allen Carlson, ("Appreciation and the Natural Environment", *Journal of Aesthetics and Art Criticism*, 37, 1979) paved the way for a very recent revival of philosophical interest in the aesthetics of nature, landscape and the environment. See, for example, Carroll, Noël "On Being Moved by Nature: Between Religion and Natural History", in Kemal, Salim and Ivan Gaskell, eds., *Landscape, Natural Beauty and the Arts*, Cambridge: Cambridge University Press, 1993; Godlovitch, Stan, "Icebreakers: Environmentalism and Natural Aesthetics", *Journal of Applied Philosophy*, 11, 1994; Carlson, Allen "Nature, Aesthetic Appreciation and Knowledge", *Journal of Aesthetics and Art Criticism*, 53, 1995; Howarth, Jane M., "Nature's Moods", *British Journal of Aesthetics*, 35, 1995; and Budd, Malcolm, "The Aesthetic Appreciation of Nature", *British Journal of Aesthetics*, 36, 1996.

13. Appleton, Jay, *Landscape in the Arts and the Sciences*, (Inaugural Lecture), University of Hull, 1980.

14. Bell, Simon and Maggie Gilvray, "A Field of Dreams", *Landscape Design*, 250, May 1996, p. 10.

15. It scarcely needs to be emphasised that, within England generally, the removal of hedgerows has reached such proportions, especially since World War II, that it has occasioned widespread concern. There are difficulties about hedgerow restoration in arable areas, since the principal reason for their initial removal, namely the inconvenience of operating large machines in small arable fields, persists. Functionally, the purpose of the hedgerow was to provide a stockproof barrier, so where stockfarming is the principal activity it is there that the restoration of hedgerows can most logically be undertaken.

16. Appleton, Jay, *Experience* pp. 190–193.

17. Stroud, Dorothy, *Humphry Repton*, London: Country Life, 1962, p. 102.

18. Pope, Alexander, An Epistle to Lord Burlington, 1731, in Dixon Hunt, John and Peter Wallis, eds., *The Genius of the Place The English Landscape Garden 1620–1820*, Cambridge Massachusetts, 1988, p. 212.

19. Grant, Bill and Paul Harris, *The Grizedale Experience: Sculpture, Arts and Theatre in a Lakeland Forest*, Edinburgh: Canongate Press, 1991.

# Motorised
# & Pasteurised

Richard Wentworth

My father was born in 1919 and in the fifties as we motored about the place he used to use this adjective 'countrified' and I always thought it was a strange, archaic term. I never knew what it meant. But he would talk about things as being countrified.

Now, thirty years later, I drive around with my own children. Through the eighties, as we motored those new, longer, smoother distances, with much greater frequency, my children would ask me "What's that in the background?" 'Background', that was the term for the landscape, for the scenography of motoring. Well, the child who coined the 'background' is now sixteen and last week I said to him "What's landscape?" and he said "It's where there's a horizon".

An image of a horizon—Teesdale. Teesdale is where I've been working on a project to define some parish boundaries. So it's a landscape that I've been spending time in and it's enough distance from London to allow oneself to think quite carefully about the state we're in.

I'd like to take you forward two hundred years because Norbury Park could be said to be two hundred years old. It might be worth remembering that the same two hundred years takes you back to the beginning of the Industrial Revolution, to the Enclosures, and also to the French Revolution. Together they take you to the beginning of our modernity.

Teesdale

In two hundred years time, should there be another conference about Norbury Park, observers might try to discuss the terms of reference in which we live today. And perhaps they will say that we were accomplished at making horizontal spaces, and how smooth and continuous these spaces were, and that possibly they were used for something called aeroplanes, but possibly sometimes as places to wait for them or to wait for other people. And they might say how immaculately we controlled these spaces, and how extremely clear the definition was.

And they would note that there were signs of our appetites and fears which we chose not to see. They would say that extreme flatness would translate into extreme smoothness and that smooth simply translated to sheen and shine and in turn to transparency, just as we may associate clear water with purity and hygiene, so our technological methods could be applied to the world around us—to make it look impervious, seamless, and reflective, wherever possible.

Our materials reach us in a variety of orthogonalised forms, and many display qualities of shine and polish which would make the ancients gasp.

Two hundreds years after Norbury Park's first birthday we continue to pictorialise things. We like to make a picture of the picture, and we like to give it edges. And we like to tell people how to see things. Boots the chemist processes thousands of glossy orthodoxies daily. The packet of holiday snaps pictorialises the world, as do the billboards in our streets and the TV in our living rooms.

They would also say that we got rid of the night, that we never had a night, and that we knew how to live continuously through the night as though it never took place. They would also say, perhaps, that two hundred years previously there had been a conference at which something was discussed which was essentially the politics of the landscape—what the landscape looks like, why it looks like it does, what it is, how we define it and so on.

Dresden

Munich

We can all understand photographs taken from the air because we've all sat at aeroplane windows and flown around places which, needless to say, two hundred years ago we would not have done. But if I told you that one image was of coming into Dresden and the other was of leaving Munich, you don't look at them in the same way. And it remains curious to me the degree to which this kind of information affects the way that one interprets how something looks, what shape it is, and how that shape was made.

Glasgow

London

Now one can extend that, of course, because we all have local landscapes. We have those little landscapes which are the most immediate surfaces. And it's surprising how many surfaces there are which actually escape the attentions of great smoothness.

So what is it that we do with the landscape? I think that what we do with the landscape is surprisingly close to kitchen units. It's another aspect of surface. It's to do with an escaped idea about hygiene, an idea now embodied in the Health and Safety at Work principles by which we're all expected to live. It's that possibility of seeing what conventionally grows on the surfaces of the earth as nothing more than carpet. You can buy it in, lay it down, take it up, remodel the surface, start again.

This obsession with surface is in everything. It's as if all our values of indoor space had escaped into the outdoors. We are sophisticated enough to distinguish public from private, and the weather still tells us which is in and which is out, but we are very busy blurring these things.

It's worth reminding ourselves that it was us who named 'nature'. It didn't name itself. So we can have tame cacti and we can have captive cats. These are all part of that game we like to play. The car may take us out into nature, but its suggestion of privacy is instantly exchanged for its public and plural version—traffic and parking. One may say we are traffic. Everything about us contributes to its character and quantity.

When this conference comes up in two hundred years, people will comment that once upon a time there was a farmhouse vernacular in which animals were kept beneath the occupants in close proximity. And they will say that after a couple of hundred years this transmogrified into the car being kept so close to the house that you could feel the warmth of the engine when you got home on a cold winter's evening. The taste and habits of the owner may even be seen to have encouraged the colour of the house to match the car, or vice-versa.

We are on a new version of the Grand Tour—it's the democratic version and the landscape is not one mediated by Poussin. Its principles, though, do originate in southern Europe. Our mental landscape is still Romanesque, one which we have mediated through the 'patio'. The fictions of the Mediterranean have migrated into a romance with Spanish/American culture. Our affair with the American South-West involves importing ideas about wilderness; the imagery is male, pioneering, and military. The Wild West has its own logical extension in the Last Frontier, out in space, American space—vehicles-named-for-the-use-of.

Frauenkirche, Dresden

In a landscape as intensely gardened as ours, penetrating the wilderness (pretend version) is an attractive game, even if the space to play in is totally unavailable.

The military realities of the twentieth century have left us with ruins of our own time. The glassed over rubble hills of Berlin or the naturalisation of the fallen cornices of the Frauenkirche in Dresden have affinities with Arcadian sites, but it's not an aesthetic error that we are likely to make; there's no comfort there. We can't go back.

Nature has escaped us, so our final solution is to try to buy it in. I doubt very much that my father would be convinced by the National Trust's countrified bottled water, 'carbonated natural spring water'—no amount of embossing with oak leaf emblems will do the trick. There is perhaps no greater contradiction at work than the double meaning of 'country'—something which might be associated with landscape, but which also may convey the nation state. Governments go to the country. Is this difficulty specific to the British English? Is the Montego Countryman fleeing the metropolis, or is it in effect a pseudonym for the Montego Brit? The other kind of country. A different kind of background.

We remain suspicious of over assertive images and nominations, while being happily seduced by the gentler ones. Our drive to pictorialise makes us sensitive to the effects of light and shade. This view is achieved by the effects of traffic. A day out in the landscape, late twentieth-century style, courtesy of Boots the chemist.

*A minute after noon; the train runs through:*
*a glimpse of distance; someone else's dreaming.*

*Quiet again. Fish listen in the weeds,*
*a pure awareness hanging in the tide:*

*each breath of wind, each voice, each grain of pollen,*
*traced and recorded; half a mile upstream*

*a kingfisher darts away*
*in the ricepaper light;*

*swallows dip and vanish in mid-air,*
*the water's sleeve*

*unravels in the sand.*
*But listen: in the furling of the stream*

*we hear the recreation of a mind*
*that will not be distracted,*

*and now is always*
*what we take on trust:*

*never the same river twice,*
*though it flows unceasing.*

# *River*

*Six Norbury Park Dreamings*
*John Burnside*

*100% Waterproof
Gortex—What to Wear in Utopia*

Tania Kovats

Tania Kovats, *Gortex*

What to wear in Utopia? A perennial question that dogs urbanites like myself. I live, by choice, in a city. Nature is therefore an idea, not a specific place that I know well. Norbury Park has no direct connection to me, nor intimate history. It is a green place, a very nice, quiet, green place, within easy reach of London, making it seem local to me.

previous page. Tania Kovats, *Imports (Knickers)*

As an artist, having been asked to consider the aesthetics of land management, I have no prescriptions. What has occurred through my encounter with Norbury Park has been a sharp focusing of how I view nature, and how that view has been culturally framed and defined.

Nature is where I go on holiday. Particularly ancient places that have been given a top dressing of modernity and turned into wilderness parks.

> The creation of the mental realm of fantasy finds a perfect parallel in the establishment of 'reservations' or 'nature reserves' in places where the requirements of agriculture, communications and industry threaten to bring about changes in the original face of the earth which will quickly make it unrecognisable. A nature reserve preserves its original state which everywhere else has to our regret been sacrificed to necessity. Everything, including what is useless and even what is noxious, can grow and proliferate there as it pleases.—Sigmund Freud[1]

I romanticise my relationship with the natural world, 'ground' myself in it. I like walking. To allow the walk to create the landscape, connecting and transforming different existing places into a unified image of an imaginary landscape.

Any Utopia requires a degree of spatial isolation in order to perfect its details and protect it from potentially corrupting influences. The contained, managed island of Norbury Park functions well as a model for such projections.

The frontiers of the island aren't the infinite oceans, rather the edge of the capital's urban sprawl: suburban borders and the hard edge of the M25.

Norbury Park's lack of signage and absence on road maps add to its Utopian condition. You have to travel to Utopia, usually to somewhere not on the map, making repeat visits impossible, but returning to the idea, or the representation of the place, essential.

I can't recommend Gortex highly enough. My two-way front zipped with raingutter flaps, rugged windproof nylon shell, Velcro closure cuffs, and fully breathable layer. Gortex waterproofs have to be the ideal choice for what to wear in Utopia.

Many other products sell themselves on how well they harmonise with the natural world. In any high street outdoor retailers there are always many open exhibitions of wet-weather fetishism to be seen. A magazine like GQ is densely populated by all-action adverts, watches sold as no-limits timing devices whether diving into water or out of a plane. Boots that will probably only see mud in a park are sold as the right choice for the rain forest.

Giotto, *St. Francis of Assisi Preaching to the Birds*

The insertion of 'nature' in the form of advertising or design, conceals the economic contradictions between urban reality and nature (which the city must exploit for its survival). 'Nature', having been ideologically dematerialised, is returned, in the world of the commercial or package design, in place of nature's actual relation to the city.—Dan Graham[2]

Surviving any weather condition allows you to take on some of the solidity of rocks and trees, so whatever happens in that big, natural playground, you stay dry. Everything is geared towards my total comfort and impermeability once I actually get to the messy wet chaos of outdoors. Every culture makes room in some way for the sacredness of nature.

The pre-modern era in Western Europe cleaved to conceptions of the world which stressed, in mystified and mystical form, the interdependence of human beings and the natural world. Christian and non-Christian alike found in natural events and phenomena the characteristics of a legible script: the world was a text which expressed intention, morality and significance. The development of industrial capitalism was accompanied by the leaching of wonder, and the percolation of disenchantment.—David Raison[3]

above, below, opposite and overleaf. Sam Raimi, *The Evil Dead*

So how does man fit into nature? You could prioritise your definitions as follows: Nature is what is neither human, nor of human origin: remote, wild, the wilderness. Or, you recognise man as part of Nature, the dominating, manipulative, exploitative part.

All landscapes that we are familiar with in this country are economies. Some economies are managed to make money; others to protect an area; some to make it more aesthetic. Nature has to be defined as a set of complex processes rather than things. Some of these originate in man's manipulation, others from the physical processes associated with the community of plants and animals that actually live there.

In our modern world various forms of politics, culture and recreation help to define our relationship with nature. Landscape is culture's code word for nature and landscape painting has centrally affected how we perceive the scene in front of us.

Other mediums—photography, TV, film, advertising and tourism—all now compete to form the framing device. The sacred status of nature is employed to re-enchant the world. Television provides a full range of magicians, from mediators like David Attenborough, a high priest of the natural world, to David Lynch with his disturbing warped projections from Twin-Peak-ed Arcadia.

Some contemporary art practice, including my own, acts as an interface in these delicate negotiations. There are obviously many possibilities, but I've selected only a few—the ones that have put in place the most persistent filters through which I experience nature.

Seeing as this is a highly subjective selection, I would first like to mention one of the most terrifying horror films I've ever watched. Embarrassingly enough, it is also a load of gory, low-budget, rubbish. The film is Sam Raimi's *The Evil Dead*.[4] A group of geeky youngsters spend the night in the woods and end up foolishly summoning up demons of the forest. One of the group wanders into the woods alone, something every woman is warned against doing. She's then subjected to the most bizarre sexual assault in which the trees bind themselves around her and attack her. The scene is one where you witness a rape, but the perpetrator of the crime is the tree that traps her on the ground and violates her.

These images had a strong impact on this impressionable 13 year old. Terrible proof of why the wood in earlier fairy stories was always such a dark and frightening place.

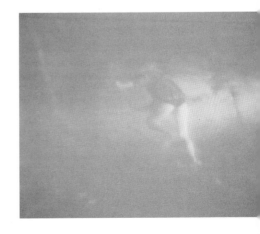

The notion that Arcadia is populated by delightful nymphs and happy farmers owes more to the Arcadian theme parks of eighteenth-century gardens and Renaissance images of nature, happily managed by the hilltop city state.

Norbury Park's Arcadian citizens are the pram-pushing mothers, joggers and employees of the theme farm. As Simon Schama points out in *Landscape and Memory*, the mark of the original Arcadians was their bestiality.[5] Their presiding divinity, Pan, copulated with goats as well as with anything else that came his way. Arcadia was a harsh and brutal landscape, difficult, testing, and far from safe.

As an artist, I have a particular interest in lost landscapes. This grew out of attempts to construct infinite non-spaces. I made a series of light installations. They were blank abstracted architecture, non-specific, site-less places. I replaced openings, doorways, or walls with walls of white light, architectural light boxes constructed with fluorescent tubes and opal perspex. These works were intended to set up an ongoing enquiry into the spiritualised ontologies of art, as well as making architectural dialogue. Their language was urban; the smooth, seamless language of the modernist white cube gallery.

This conversation has turned towards landscape or nature over the last couple of years. These works are exports from nature. I do not actually work in the landscape.

Tania Kovats, *Grotto*

Initially I made *Grotto*. This was meant as a location for the Virgin Mary who I see as another kind of Utopian place or site, and the most important female archetype in western culture. This is about a perfect place, a place on earth closest to heaven. In this piece I offer no resistance to the status of the classical grotto as gateway to the underworld. *Grotto* is housed in a white plinth which creates a theatrical collision between nature and culture.

Other landscape pieces have followed. These refer to very spiritualised, aesthetic landscapes. None are specific. They are generic landscapes, lifted from holy dramas or sites of transfigurations.

Tania Kovats, *Landscape III: Cave*

Tania Kovats, *Ledge*

*The Cave*, the most fundamental manifestation of shelter or architecture. The *Tomb*. The mountain *Retreat*. The *Canyon*. Landscapes of awe, rather than the picturesque.

One piece, called *Ledge*, refers to a mountainous rocky outcrop, an elemental landscape, but always in a fake kind of way.

Tania Kovats, *Landscape II: Tomb*

Tania Kovats, *Canyon*

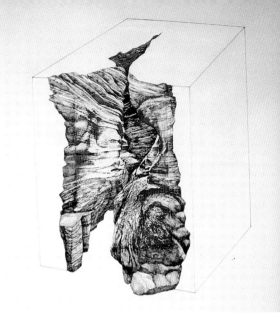

above & below. Tania Kovats, *Rocky Outcrop*

Mountains are culturally established as the ultimate site of heroic human triumph, with an invented relationship between altitude and omniscience. Climbing a mountain involves a complex polarisation and union of physical and mental stress. In all these works the palpable absence of man is supposed to be suggested, while simultaneously man's presence is implied.

Tania Kovats, *Imports,(Glue Sniffing)*

Norbury Park may not be the sort of visionary landscape full of exhilarating physical challenges, high points, gorges, bungee jumping, etc., with extremes of climate or terrain, but it is strangely possible to achieve isolation there. You are rarely out of earshot from traffic, or far from a path, but you can walk alone, which has to be one of its most attractive features.

Tania Kovats, *Imports, (One Shoe)*

Tania Kovats, *Imports (Pornography)*

But you are never anywhere that somebody else hasn't been before you—again the palpable presence of absent man. Everyone will have had the disturbing experience of finding certain remnants of that presence whilst walking in Arcadia. This interrupts the 'communing with nature' and interrupts the intersection of pleasure and adrenaline.

Imports to Norbury Park: the discomfort of finding abandoned knickers; discarded glue sniffing equipment; the unsettling mystery of seeing just one shoe; or distress at finding condom litter and used pornography. And worst of all, the tent erected over where they find the body.

Tania Kovats, *Imports (Condom)*

Gregory Crewdson, *Untitled*

Gregory Crewdson is a stalker. He stalks his own silk feather and balsa wood created worlds. The American-born artist's subject is the lost Utopia of suburbia, the jewel of white heterosexual culture, a showcase for the family, the safe, enclosed world, shut off from poverty and unruly nature. He takes photographs of model, miniature environments. A pretty horde of beetles engulfs an unknown length of something, stripping it of meat, or bark, in such a dense frenzy that they might actually start eating each other.

Peace and quiet creep across the background of these cul-de-sac communities, whilst nature teems in nauseous abundance in the foreground. Like strange, dead still lives, these images borrow from the climate of Spielberg's suburbia, a world prone to insuppressible invasion, and perhaps owe even more to the bizarre opening sequence of David Lynch's *Blue Velvet*.

Man is represented by architecture, one of humanity's major strategies for protection from nature. The architecture of suburbia always seem sinisterly quiet, with evidence that someone has put up defences against, or is manipulating nature.[6]

**BLIND SPOT**

Willie Doherty, *Blindspot*

A very different, but equally resonant, wall of defences is set up in the work of the Northern Irish artist Willy Doherty. His work explores the demarcation of territory. The *Nature Disorders* series parodies the photographic text work of Richard Long and Hamish Fulton and forces a problematic recognition of the role nature plays in an urban war zone.

Landscape is not neutral or transparent, but is rather a deeply encoded text where rights of ownership, myth, identity and nationhood are inscribed.

The installation, *the only good one is a dead one*, is a double screen video production. On one screen the artist uses a hand-held video camera to record a night-time car journey. The second shows the view from inside a car which is stationary and parked on a suburban street. These images are accompanied by a soundtrack of an interior monologue where an Irish male voice goes back and forth between his fear of being the victim of, and his fantasy of being, an assassin.

# BARBARIC MIRE

## WEEPING

Willie Doherty, *Barbaric Mire—Weeping*

Set against the intensity of the monologue, the film of the winding country road at the edge of the city seems to utterly intrude on the possibilities of isolated pleasures in Arcadia. Night-driving produces a tunnel of light and visibility and a great mass of blind shifting darkness. In the real darkness of the installation space your own identify shifts to pace that of the speaker. The paranoia of the streaming monologue cannot help but saturate you with anxiety. Despite its banality, something terrifying is about to happen. It's the instinct that makes you check the dark back seat of your car, or worry that something unexpected will jump out from the dark sides of the road. An instinct so familiar, but targeted so precisely in this work.

A work that I consciously recognise as having framed my experience of landscape is a piece by Graham Gussin, called *Meeting (Number 1)*. No matter how far I travel, how much my head clears, how far I walk before setting up camp for the night, unbeknown to me I've taken this image with me. It is an image of the perfect moment. We all have our own definitions or memory of the perfect moment. I get a lot of my oceanic experiences when I walk in remote places. Peak experiences are constantly being sold and fed to us, every time we turn on the TV or look at a magazine. Why else is it that committed ex-smokers insist on a cigarette when they get to the top of the mountain?

So, this image. Everything is just right. The delicious tiredness of a day's walking with a pack on your back, the immature and primitive delight of building a fire to cook on with someone I love, and for once to feel saturated with the fleeting sensation of having arrived, because that's where you are, that's how far today got you. A moment of full gestalt sensation.

I blink, and this image pops up. What is happening is an acting out of something already represented. All I'm doing is shifting into frame.

Notes

1   Freud, Sigmund, *Introductory Lectures on Psychoanalysis,* Trans. James Strachy, eds., Strachy, James and Angela Richards, Harmondsworth: Penguin, 1976, p. 419.

2   Graham, Dan, "Video View of Suburbia in an Urban Atrium (1979-1980)", *Rock My Religion: Writings and Projects 1965-1990,* Cambridge Massachsetts: The MIT Press, 1993.

3   Raison, David, "Hard Singing of Country", *Unpainted Landscape,* Edinburgh: Scottish Arts Council, 1987.

4   *The Evil Dead,* written and directed by Sam Raimi, Palace/Renaissance Production, USA, 1980 (released 1983).

5   Schama, Simon, *Landscape and Memory,* New York: Harper Collins, 1995.

6   Schorr, Collier, "Close Encounters", *Frieze,* March/April 1995.

Graham Gussin, *Meeting (Number 1)*

# Norbury Park:
# The View from London

Ken Worpole

Modern geography is no longer about distances so much as personal worlds and experiences; not spatial, but cultural. The maps that people use today are inside their heads rather than held awkwardly in their hands. The relationship between space and time is increasingly fluid, as any traveller who has spent two hours crossing London to get to Heathrow in order to spend an hour and fifty minutes travelling to Stockholm will know.

previous page. Phoenix Park, London

In one of the more original travel books of recent years, *Roissey Express* by François Maspero, the writer spent almost a month travelling on a single Paris suburban train line, getting off at every station to stay the night, talk to people and get a feel of how people lived.[1] He was never more than fifteen miles from his own apartment, but stayed away from home for nearly a month in order to experience fully the distances and deep interiors of the *bidonvilles*. One of his most bitter criticisms of suburban planning and transport policy was that it could take up to three hours to get from one suburban or district centre to the next by public transport, a journey which by car could be accomplished in ten minutes. Maspero also describes many of the blighted public housing projects he visited as "landscape delivered in bulk".

One more example to illustrate this point. A friend of mine, a transport consultant, described how it was easier to get from Southall to Wolverhampton than from Southall to most other parts of London, simply because, as each contained a large Sikh community, there was a dedicated, regular, daily coach service linking the two places. We have overlaid the physical world with cultural networks which often bear little relation to physical communications.

What these introductory remarks suggest, I hope, is that the relationship between London and Norbury Park is no longer about distance (if it ever was) or a pure set of polarities such as city/country or urbanity/nature, but about cultural maps and landscapes which people have created, for themselves and others, but which can also be moulded, creatively or positively, by different agencies, or manipulated to achieve other ends. In short, our geographical and cultural world is constructed, not given.

## Town and Country

The way forward for Norbury Park cannot be separated from much larger arguments about the changing relationship between town and country. This relationship, now fraught with difficulties, is the subject of increasingly powerful lobby groups with political pressures being exerted from both sides.

The principal cause of pressure is an apparent disillusionment among city-dwellers with the quality of modern urban life. People fear street crime, worry about pollution and the health of their children, and view with increasing dismay the ageing infrastructure of services around them: pre-war schools, nineteenth-century hospitals, Carnegie libraries, Victorian parks fraying at the edges, privatised corporation buses churning out diesel fumes, boarded up department stores and shuttered high streets. What they want are out-of-town shopping malls easily accessible by car, multi-facility 'leisure boxes' built on green field sites, country parks with car parks and interpretation centres, and modern schools to which their children can walk in safety. The 1995 *Park Life* report, of which I was co-author, showed that city-dwellers with cars preferred to visit a country park or out-of-town garden centre at the weekend rather than walk to their local park. [2]

The Council for the Protection of Rural England (CPRE) report, *Leisure Landscapes*, published in 1994, detailed the scale of the urban invasion into the countryside, noting that 45% of all car journeys are now made for leisure purposes.[3] The CPRE report showed how great the pressures on the countryside are in terms of active sports and recreation, as leisure and tourism based jobs replace agricultural jobs, and leisure woodlands and golf courses take up set-aside arable land. In 1950 there were 700,000 agricultural workers; today there are just 200,000. Only 6% of rural workers are now employed in agriculture. The very notion of a working landscape, of rural life as a productive agricultural life, is now under siege as the Common Agricultural Policy and discretionary leisure spending combine to turn the countryside into a playground, heritage trail, or site for new kinds of expensive housing estates, confirming that urban and rural problems are becoming increasingly interlocked. These pressures have been referred to time and again in the discussions about Norbury Park.

As was obvious at the 1995 National Trust centenary conference (a watershed of public heart-searching and self-criticism), an increasing part of the Trust's work in managing its rural sites and properties is in reducing rather than increasing visitors. As a body, the National Trust is quietly powerful, not just in terms of its two million membership, but also in its extensive ownership of land and organisational strength. It could, if it so wished, park a lot of metaphorical tanks on other people's lawns, including the government's. It was also evident at the conference that the National Trust now has its eye on the urban heritage and a keen interest in urban issues. Significantly, the Countryside Commission is also beginning to make inroads into urban planning policy and has lately published a report on Urban Trees, while its offshoot, the Groundwork Trust, now largely works in urban areas on derelict land reclamation. Even more provocative perhaps, was the recent launch by the CPRE of its *Urban Footprints* campaign, calling for increased urban consolidation under the slogan 'The future of our countryside depends on our towns and cities treading more lightly on the environment'. More recently, the Countryside Movement, a well-funded, but apparently ad hoc alliance of agri-business, hunting, and other rural interests, has embarked on a public campaign to educate city-dwellers in the realities of rural life, while covertly attacking the animal rights movement, vegetarianism, anti-roads protesters, and other 'misinformed' people who are seen to pose a threat to what is going on at Cold Comfort Farm, now that the battery cages and the twenty-four hour artificial lighting systems have been installed.

The sub-text of these policies and campaigns could be thought to suggest, be it ever so gently, that city-dwellers should stay where they belong. Suddenly, in Britain, it seems that we are getting to a ridiculous situation where urban policy is being developed, by default, by rural pressure groups, some of which are keen to ensure that the urban masses stay put in their city enclaves. Cynics might also detect a degree of opportunism in the way in which rural and landed interests are wrapping themselves in the green flag and claiming environmental reasons for keeping the countryside free of outside intruders.

There is, however, little that can prevent the urban rich from buying into rural life, rather than simply visiting it. The modern village or market-town, certainly in the South East, is becoming a dormitory settlement as people work in the city but go home at night to their version of the rural idyll. It was ever thus according to the historian Martin Wiener, whose book *English Culture and the Decline of the Industrial Spirit* notes how frequently the industrial masters moved to join the rural aristocracy once they had made their pile.[4] The urge to leave Albert Square or Coronation Street to live in Ambridge still seems a pervasive ingredient of the English dream. The only people who claim to love cities are the families and children of immigrants who have settled here. When I interviewed the Guyana-born novelist Mike Phillips, for a Radio 4 *Analysis* programme in 1995, he was effusive about the magnetism of the city: "You must understand", he told me, "we never had the myth of a rural paradise. We embraced the city because it meant progress, material progress, intellectual progress, educational progress".[5] The positive contribution that ethnic minority communities have made to British urban life remains largely unacknowledged. But this surely should not mean that Britain's ethnic minority populations should not have the same rights of access to the countryside as other city-dwellers, even if the black presence in the countryside is still currently viewed with alarm in some quarters, and the countryside is still felt by many black people to be dangerous territory.[6]

The fact is that Norbury Park has a historic-cultural (and economic) relationship with London. It is as it is because of key urban policy interventions in the form of the Metropolitan Green Belt policy and general London support for the County Council purchase of the estate from private hands in 1931. At the time of purchase Norbury Park would have potentially been regarded as a future resource for Londoners; a place to visit, a place in which to seek tranquillity in an era in which the motor car, through advertising and other imagery, was seen as an increasingly organic part of the countryside experience. Alison Light and Mark Linardo, among other social historians, have addressed the representation of the car in the natural setting in the imagery of the roadside picnic, the rolling country lane with its single, open-topped sports car, and the car park at the beauty spot disgorging dozens of happy families.[7] Norbury Park might well have been the site of such a roadside idyll between the wars. Yet today, there is a deep ambivalence whether Norbury Park exists as a resource for Londoners. As Eileen O'Keefe points out elsewhere in this collection, the poor public transport links and the minimal road sign-posting, combined with the hidden jewel sensibility which is attached to the site, all contribute to a kind of exclusion zone, intentional or not.

## Public Access and the Nature of the Modern Public

The argument so far takes for granted the public access status of Norbury Park. Public access and public rights of way are part of the folklore of the countryside, though interestingly, less so of the modern city where—with hardly a murmur of dissent—many public rights of way have been ceded to private developments, particularly as a result of the creation of enclosed shopping malls. But definitions of the 'public' in modern discourse are now deeply problematic, especially with regard to the nature of public goods, public service and universal provision in an age of free market solutions and the triumph of the sovereign consumer. Defending public goods—generally paid for by compulsory taxation and provided universally, irrespective of individual benefit or use—has become increasingly difficult. Norbury Park is a classic case of public good being paid for by millions of tax-payers and used by only thousands. Does it matter? For after all, the regular users of Norbury Park (and it is unhelpful that we know so little about them, although knowledge of their social status and demographic profile could weaken the case) also pay taxes to support other public goods—libraries, sports centres, swimming pools, social services—which they may not use. Once you open up the debate about the economic equitability of public goods you really do open a can of worms and can end up like spoiled children arguing over tokens at the end of a game of snakes and ladders.

CCTV Cameras at Pallister Park, Middlesbrough

Public goods are regarded as the staples of a basic quality of life in advanced, democratic, and relatively wealthy societies, and have a number of particular attributes. They are usually provided universally and are open to all with no entry requirements, whether we are considering roads, schools, museums, libraries, parks, child benefit, access to health care and so on. They have traditionally been provided free, although people do now pay for medical prescriptions, for entry into sports centres, and fairly recently—and contentiously—for entry into some museums. They often inhabit a distinct architectural style or built form, be it neo-classical town halls, libraries and museums, or distinctive kinds of frame-buildings which define post-war schools, health centres, etc. It is never difficult to identify public buildings even in an unfamiliar townscape. Lastly, for the purposes of this essay, public goods have often prescribed certain modes of behaviour such as the rule of silence in the library (still there in some form after more than a hundred years, and still appreciated by users as contributing to the sanctuary atmosphere of the public library), school rules and school discipline, or the by-laws of parks. Indeed, the layout of parks has often been expressly designed to provide maximum public cross-surveillance.[8] Public goods are provided as part of a social contract.

Today, many of these historic attributes are now in question. The wealthier sections of society have increasingly—and some always have—bought their education, leisure, health and culture in the private market-place, but more and more people are doing so now. There is talk of targeting some welfare benefits (for example, child benefit, pensions), rather than providing them universally as of old. Museums have imposed charges and other public services, such as leisure centres, have been encouraged, if not forced, to charge market prices for admission. Museum charges have raised some interesting questions regarding the relationship between social equity and fiscal virtue. A recent commentator on the issues raised by voluntary entry charges being introduced at the Victoria and Albert Museum noted that "The tax-payer subsidised each visit to the V & A by £14 before they introduced a voluntary charge. Afterwards each visit cost us £24, because the level of attendance fell so much".[9]

Leon Kossoff, *Children's Swimming Pool*, 1971

The elasticity of the relationship between entry charges and numbers of users is still a conundrum for local government finance and public goods theory. Is it preferable to raise income but reduce numbers and subsidise each visitor more, or spend more but secure greater value for money in subsidy terms? There is now even talk of charging for new roads, or even specific lanes on existing roads. Clearly, there will be other proposals to impose charges on services traditionally thought to have been universal and free. One result of this is that the 'public' as a unified concept is considerably weakened and increasingly revealed to be made up of distinct sub-groups, classes, or specific communities; each of which may need to be treated differently, on the old Aristotelian principal that equals should be treated equally and unequals unequally.

Consequently, the world becomes one of concessionary pricing schemes, differential pricing, differentiated forms of access and so on. The public swimming pool is a paradigm of this process. Originally there was a standard price for adults and a standard price for children, often of a token nature. As swimming pools contributed to improved public health, it was felt that local authorities should only impose minimal charging policies. Most sessions were open sessions. Saturday afternoon at the municipal pool was often a war of all against all, as Leon Kossoff's marvellous paintings show. Adults, children, good swimmers, novices, all had to take their chance in the general public *mêlée*. More recently, a new ethos has prevailed which understands that serious swimmers are best separated off from beginners, children at times from adults, men from women, pensioners from teenagers and so on. The public, in short, is made up of a number of distinct needs and interests.

We now seem to be a long way from the problems of Norbury Park, but bear with me. For what the swimming pool paradigm demonstrates is that you can allow universal access to a facility, for free or charged, but regulate use and convenience to users in other ways, in this case by time separation or dividing access up into distinct time zones. Thus everybody gets a right to use the facility, but without the conflicts of need and interest which arise out of an unregulated open access policy. Parks are classic examples of public facilities in which conflicts between users are always present in some form or other, most notably in the quite different interests of dog-owners and the parents of young children. But there are other conflicts of use, between cyclists and the elderly and infirm, between people who wish to play games using hard balls and casual walkers, between those who seek solitude and quiet and those who want the park to be a main site for local pop festivals, between those who want the park open at night and those who want it closed, between the ecologists who want to see the mown grass revert to meadowland and those who admire the dignity and order of the shorn grass and carpet bedding, between the heritage interests who want to reinstate the traditional railings, footpaths and structured planting, and those who want roller-blading areas and baseball courts. These conflicts will never be finally resolved, but what is most interesting is how people still successfully negotiate their own needs and uses of the urban park with others without reverting to litigation, violence or sullen withdrawal.[10]

opposite. Girl Guides at Norbury Park, 1941

## New Forms of Regulation in the Public Sphere

There are moves, however, to re-think issues of public access to parks and open spaces in more imaginative and creative ways which do recognise conflicts of interest, and these are highly germane to the debate about the future of Norbury Park. In a number of North American city parks, for example, the conflicts over irresponsible dog ownership and the inconvenience to other park users caused by dog fouling, or aggressive dogs running loose, have been partly addressed by time-zoning. Dogs are allowed off their leads only before 9am and even then they are still restricted to certain areas. Similar discussions are going on in some of the London parks as to how to regulate cycling in parks which many park users regard as anti-social and dangerous. One suggestion is that cycling is permitted only in the morning and early evening to allow people using bikes to commute to work, but preventing casual bike use throughout the day.

But open spaces are obviously less amenable to time-zoning than to other forms of regulation, either in the form of restricted access or restricted uses. Restricted access is, rightly, difficult to impose on public space, the origins of which go back to the 'commons'.[11] Yet in our several studies of urban parks we have come across

parks which, owned and administered by trusts rather than public bodies, can impose their own entry criteria, for example, Coram's Fields in Bloomsbury, London, which only allows in adults accompanying children. This exclusion of lone adults was designed to allay the fears of local parents who thought it would make the park safer for children—it is essentially a play park—and this practice does seem to work. In similar ways, London's Royal Parks, and indeed the Corporation of London's parks, are much more rule-governed than local authority parks, as specific parliamentary legislation is granted to these more august bodies to impose restrictions on use.

The main forms of regulation, though, are restrictions on use or activity, and in this respect Norbury Park is already covered by many forms of covenant. Primarily, of course, it is part of the Green Belt which automatically disallows the possibility of planning permission being granted for development. It is also part of an Area of Outstanding Natural Beauty, as well as a Site of Special Scientific Interest, and is seeking to be further designated a Special Area for Conservation under the European Habitats Directive and an Area of Historic Landscape Value within the County Council's Countryside Strategy. It will soon have more letters after its name than a Chief Admiral. All these forms of designation place more and more restrictions on what can and cannot be done in the park and most people will be in favour of such forms of regulation (while at the same time some of those, perhaps a little hypocritically, will remain in favour of the deregulation of everything else in the social and institutional life of the culture).[12] In this way, space becomes highly differentiated and regulated, no longer dichotomised simply between private or public, but layered with all kinds of covenants, qualifications, and restrictions.

Forms of designation and zoning are also at work in the modern town and city, sometimes for the good, but sometimes with fairly dubious or even pernicious implications. It is worth looking at some of these new zoning types because they are relevant to Norbury Park. Urban zoning is synonymous with the development of town planning in Britain and the era of architectural modernism associated with Le Corbusier and the *La Ville Radieuse*, with its quite distinct and separate, residential, commercial, and industrial areas. Land use planning is still the dominant mode of designating appropriate uses for urban space, although as a result of some kinds of deregulation of use-classes it is now much easier to mix residential with light industrial, and so on.

One of the most successful forms of urban zoning in recent years has been the designation of conservation areas in many places; areas in which the historic character of the townscape and its individual buildings are preserved by a set of restrictions on possible demolition or inappropriate developments and embellishments, and where funding is available to help individual householders and business owners preserve or restore original features. The Civic Trust has been very active in supporting these kinds of conservationist policies. At the opposite end of the zoning spectrum we have seen the growth of 'enterprise zones' in areas of blighted ex-industrial land with high unemployment and little amenity, in which investment is encouraged "through the streamlining and simplification of planning procedures and administrative controls, and through the introduction of fiscal advantages (exemptions against rates and capital allowances) for companies in Enterprise Zone sites".[13] The concept of enterprise zones developed out of earlier 'assisted areas' and 'derelict land grant' schemes, both of which were targeted at specific areas of urban decline. The most recent government initiative, City Challenge, is also highly specific in its spatial definitions of eligibility.

These forms of urban zoning are largely benign and are about encouraging development, activity and use. In North America, however, where urban policy is at present sharper and more brutal—while remembering that we continue to take many British leads from it—urban zoning has a distinctly exclusionary bite to it. The expert witness on these trends is Mike Davis who has studied zoning policy in great detail and has identified the worrying link between architecture and law enforcement, whereby the police often have the final say in matters of urban design, for example vetoing proposals to provide public toilets in parks and subway stations.[14] American cities now contain 'abatement districts', 'enhancement districts', 'containment zones' and 'exclusion zones', each of which marries a certain kind of social control policy to land use regulation, principally around issues of drink, drugs, sleeping rough, and loitering. The argument is not that anti-social behaviour is to be approved of, but rather that this kind of blanket regulation effectively takes away people's individual civil rights, and further marginalises and criminalises those who already feel themselves excluded from the public realm.

Spatial regulation can succeed only if it is legitimated by public understanding and approval. This is linked to whether people feel their considerations are taken seriously and that they have a stake in the successful management of these invaluable public spaces. The vocabulary of 'ownership' or 'stakeholding' is relevant here. Not knowing very much about the current users of Norbury Park in terms of who they are and where they come from—and I think this kind of profiling is essential to good management—we can only surmise that most of them are fairly local. There is also some impressionistic evidence that these people regard Norbury Park as their park and, wishing to retain its identity as a hidden jewel known only to a select few, resent visitors from further afield. Legal ownership, of course, resides with Surrey County Council, which may well wish to see Norbury Park promoted to a wider Surrey catchment group of potential users. But there again, it can be argued that Surrey County Council own and manage it in trust for the nation—it is after all part of what is arguably a national area of outstanding natural beauty. One cannot be parochial about these things. Even national institutions have to be located somewhere and have a local identity. The vocabulary of stake-holding may be more relevant than legal or moral ownership. Clearly Surrey County Council which owns it, the professional staff who manage it and work in it, all have a significant stake in its successful future. But its particular ecological value also makes it a site of special interest to ecologists, environmentalists and educationalists, who regard it as an invaluable resource for understanding bio-diversity and therefore should be regarded as significant stake-holders too.

A totally open door policy devoted to maximising use of Norbury Park would in fact destroy the very thing that makes it unique and so distinctive, and therefore there are very strong arguments for regulating use and the kinds of activities that could be allowed on the site, in the interests of its long term viability. In a rather outdated political belief system and vocabulary, we are of course talking about rationing. There would have to be a very strong and convincing rationale for restricting use while at the same time promoting the unique character and value of the site. Just letting it remain a resource only for those 'in the know' is not sufficient justification for the spending of public money on a site that in most senses belongs to everybody, in the long tradition of the commons.

In this respect I would agree with Jane Howarth (whose paper is printed within this collection) that the educational value of Norbury Park is perhaps its pre-eminent value, and that it might be interesting to declare the park a Site of Special Educational & Environmental Interest, or some such other designation, promoting it specifically for *bona fide* educational and environmental group visits from schools and colleges not just in Surrey, but from elsewhere in the region too, including of course London. If you wish to prohibit trail bikes, mountain bikes, barbecues, or other uses inimical to the ecology of the park, then there has to be some justification. In my experience, people do respect forms of regulation where the reasoning behind the regulation makes it quite clear that other uses have to be prioritised. What many people do not like is a long list of rules and regulations which seem arbitrary and potentially motivated by a sense of exclusion for exclusion's sake.

I have dealt at length with the more general issues of public access and the nature of public goods in this contribution because I feel them to be at the heart of the wider debates emerging from Agenda 21, and exhortations for people to subscribe to greater environmental, economic and social sustainability.[15] It is the latter issue which interests me most. How do we encourage people to respect each other's different needs and interests, particularly in relation to goods and services held in common? The world we live in now is so very different from that Victorian world in which so many of these public goods—parks, libraries, museums, schools—were first established. The modern world is much more individualistic, as well as being much more culturally diverse, and perhaps fragmented. There is no longer a unified public or an easily agreed set of assumptions about what public provision should be. This was our major finding about urban park development between the wars which seemed to be based on the principles of utilitarianism and standardisation.[16] Every large scale public space will need to secure its own unique future, based on close observation of use, responsiveness to need, and informed by the principles of stewardship and future sustainability. No more "landscape delivered in bulk", as Maspero rightly protested.

I personally believe that the future values of society will be very much tied up with the way we value and cherish the public realm and I am very grateful for the opportunity to visit Norbury Park, to talk to those who know it much better than I ever will, and to share ideas with other people interested in these issues; all of which has helped me to see much more clearly the crucial importance of these new ways of valuing the things we hold in common.

## Notes

1 Maspero, François, *Roissey Express*, London: Verso, 1995.

2 Greenhalgh, Liz & Ken Worpole, *Park Life: Urban Parks & Social Renewal*, London: Comedia/Demos, 1995.

3 *Leisure Landscapes: Leisure, Culture and the English Countryside: Challenges & Conflicts*, Council for the Protection of Rural England (CPRE), 1994.

4 Wiener, Martin, *English Culture and the Decline of the Industrial Spirit*, Cambridge: Cambridge University Press, 1981.

5 "Do European Cities Have a Future?", *Analysis*, Radio 4, 19 October 1995.

6 Young, Lola, "Environmental Images and Imaginary Landscapes", *Soundings*, No. 1, Autumn 1995.

7 Light, Alison, *Forever England: Femininity, Literature and Conservatism between the Wars*, London: Routledge, 1991. Also Linardo, Mark, *Car, Culture and the Countryside Change*, London: National Trust, 1996.

8 For the public library ethos see Greenhalgh, Liz & Ken Worpole with Charles Landry, *Libraries in a World of Cultural Change*, London: UCL Press, 1995. For a clear account of the way in which early public park layout was designed to modify and 'improve' behaviour see Taylor, Hilary, *Age and Order: The Public Park as a Metaphor for a Civilised Society*, London: Comedia Working Paper, 1995.

9 Spalding, Julian, "How to Commit Curatorial Suicide", *The Guardian*, 21 September 1996.

10 Obviously country parks and large tracts of open countryside are also the subject of many conflicts between users, and this is one of the main themes of the CPRE Leisure Landscapes report—see note 3.

11 The debate about the relevance of 'the commons' as a legal form and model of collective rights has recently been revived in a period of intense anxiety over the impact of technology on intellectual property rights. See Frow, John, "Information as Gift and Property", *New Left Review*, No. 219, 1996, and more exhaustively, Thompson, E. P., "Custom, Law and Common Right", *Customs in Common*, Harmondsworth: Penguin, 1993.

12 There are a number of other ways in which the British countryside is being demarcated in the interests of social and environmental policy including the Countryside Commission's recent work on defining 'Tranquil Areas' as well as the National Trust's work in designating coastal areas of outstanding merit.

13 *Assessing the Impact of Urban Policy*, London: Department of the Environment, HMSO, 1994, p. 98.

14 Davis, Mike, *Beyond Blade Runner: Urban Control and the Ecology of Fear*, New Jersey: The Open Magazine Pamphlet Series, 1994.

15 Agenda 21 was the name given to the programme—agreed at the 1992 Rio Earth Summit—under which national and local government in all of the signatory countries would endeavour to create plans for sustainable development in future, recognising the need to conserve the planet's natural resources.

16 Greenhalgh & Worpole, *Park Life*.

*Out of the wind, in the green*
*shadow of a thorn,*

*a glimpse of deer or fox between the leaves,*      *the fern-light*
*then nothing:*      *in the shadow of the bridge,*

*but the mind needs nothing more*      *a footpath blurring out*
*for wilderness:*      *in fog or rain,*

      *a stand of balsam.*
      *Children go home with pockets full of chalk,*

*beech-mast and feathers,*
*snail shells and sycamore wings,*

*and what they will remember is a moment's*
*pause, between The Scrubs*

*and Druid's Grove:*
*the smell of pasture gusted through the trees,*

*a slant of light,*
*the mystery of being.*

# Childhood

Six Norbury Park Dreamings
John Burnside

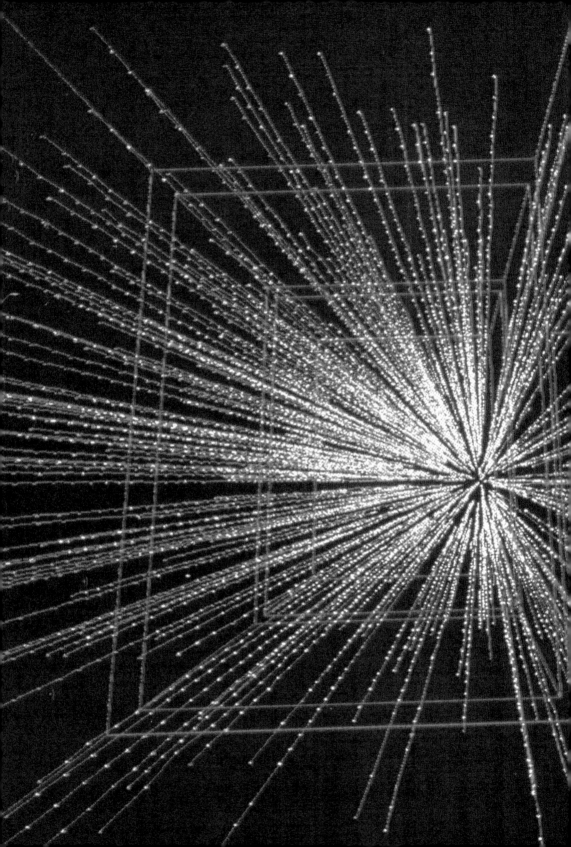

# A Railway
# Runs Through It

Jane Howarth

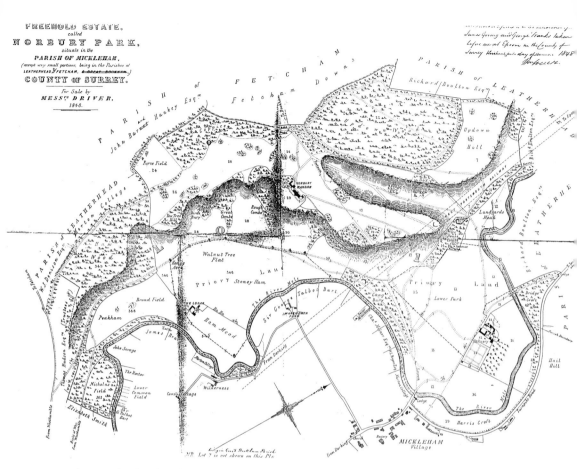

Map showing railway line through Norbury Park, 1848

Readers familiar with Norbury Park will know that a railway line does indeed run through it, not just in the ordinary sense of running across it, over its surface, but at one point runs underground through a tunnel. This is not because there was a hill too high for trains to climb, but because a railway line would have spoilt the view for the local gentry from the grand house. So a hill was built to cover it.

previous page. Lead ion collisions

What does this story suggest? It suggests many divisions: between country and city, rich and poor, beauty and use, leisure and work; but underlying these divisions, the integration of nature and artifice. Artifice was used to disguise artifact, to construct what would in time become natural again, a hill.

This particular story evokes, more generally, the story of Norbury Park, a park that has a long and varied history of all manner of interactions between people and nature—productive, exploitative, aesthetic, sensitive, insensitive, respectful, disrespectful. There is a story to be told. The question is how do we want the story to continue, how do we want Norbury Park to go on into the twenty-first century, the next millennium.

Norbury Park was purchased by Surrey County Council in 1931 when the point of preserving green areas may have been more obvious. The current concern over Norbury Park perhaps reflects an uncertainty about what the park is and what it is which is to be protected. It is no longer enough simply to say that it is green. Appeals are made to heritage, to rare species, to habitats, to old yew trees, but why are such things worth saving? At the end of the current millennium we are in danger of losing sight of two things: our capacity to contemplate and appreciate nature as our natural home, and our capacity to develop and refine our initial likes and dislikes. Norbury Park provides an opportunity to re-activate these capacities.

In this century we have come to regard nature both as a raw material to exploit and as a resource for our pleasure. It is presented as a commodity, as an instrument for our use. But nature does not exist just to be used, as though it were of mere instrumental value, in principle replaceable by artifacts. It is to be appreciated and valued in a much deeper way. However much is built, it is still nature in which we as human beings fundamentally dwell. Unspoilt places such as Norbury Park can enable us to experience a deep and respectful appreciation of nature as something other than an instrument for our use.

So there is the problem of having little nature left to value as anything other than an instrument, but there is also the danger of having little or no capacity left for valuing the nature we have. Now that might seem acceptable, so long as nature can support human life and supply our needs. But put so starkly, there is surely something wrong. Perhaps future generations with no experience of wild nature would not consciously miss it and maybe no-one would be dissatisfied, but they might be worse off and their lives might be less rich. Had Beethoven never lived we would not miss his music, but we should be deprived of much delight and wonder and our lives would be poorer. The good life for humans includes valuing nature, experiencing the awe and wonder it can create.

Anyone seeking to put such a case for the value of nature and the value of appreciating it is likely to face a problem. They will be construed as simply voicing a personal preference. It is very much a feature of late twentieth-century life that when one tries to have a reasoned discussion about a subject which touches on value, sooner or later someone will interject that everyone is entitled to their opinion, for values are subjective. This move is often made quite sincerely in a spirit of tolerance and liberalism. Its effect, however, is the very reverse; it silences discussion. It involves a refusal to engage, a failure to listen to other people and to take the character of their attachments seriously, and a reluctance to understand the basis of their appreciation. If we do not listen to each other or seek to articulate our own values we risk losing them, allowing them to deteriorate, to become at best trivial, at worst decadent.

The aim is to improve Norbury Park, to make it better. Consequently, we are operating in the area of values, not just facts. So let us try to establish what values are. Values, be they social, political, moral or aesthetic, are increasingly treated and spoken of as if they were matters of personal, subjective preference, of likes and dislikes. In this way values are turned into facts about what people happen to like. In the environmental field generally these preferences are then translated into cash terms by asking people how much they would or would not pay for a proposed change. This produces a figure which can get onto the balance sheet for a cost benefit analysis. This is economically convenient, but as a way of assessing whether a proposed change is an improvement, this procedure is highly dubious. Values are not just preferences. Some preferences are not just likes or dislikes. Cash is not an appropriate way of reflecting either values or serious preferences. Some values are better than others, some preferences deeper, more informed.

No doubt we can all think of cases when our preferences have been transformed from shallow to deep: we have moved from being superficially attracted to something to loving, respecting and valuing it, and our lives have thereby been enriched. And it is that profound, important sort of valuing which we as a culture are losing sight of, at least in public decision-making. This sort of transformation—from mere likes to profound values—typically involves enhancing one's sensitivity to what one comes to value: one develops skills of 'reading', of knowing, and of interacting respectfully with what one comes to value. Preferences are transformed, made richer, better, by knowledge which feeds into perception and stimulates the imagination. Aesthetic appreciation of art or nature is one central area where this sort of transformation happens. We start with Little Miss Muffet—Delius or Hardy take a little longer. Spectacular sunsets have an immediate appeal, limestone pavements may be an acquired taste.

The late twentieth century is, however, a difficult time to be heard. If we do manage to convince others that we are not speaking of a purely personal preference for something, but of a deeper appreciation which is life-enhancing, the subsequent charge will likely be that we are being elitist. The charge will be that it is somehow politically incorrect to suggest that great literature is better than nursery rhymes, or that lengthy, patient absorption in a natural scene is better than taking a quick snapshot and moving on. So, are those who appreciate natural places being elitist, or is it rather that those who do not are philistines? If by elitist one is referring to the possession of an intimate knowledge of something which informs and produces a richer experience, what is wrong with being elitist? What is the alternative?—no education at all? Is it elitist to be able to read what is going on at a football match? It is certainly a sport where one has to learn the rules to appreciate fully, but once mastered they enhance appreciation of the game enormously. Few would deem that elitist. Having abilities to discern, discriminate or appreciate, which not everyone has, is not bad in itself.

It is elitist, and perniciously so however, if others are excluded from an experience by being deprived of the means to learn, appreciate and understand what is there to be valued. If the love of nature is exclusive because of a shortage of natural places or a lack of education concerning them, then that is scarcely the fault of those who do appreciate them and seek to protect them. It is, however, the responsibility of developers who destroy natural places and limit the opportunities people have to enjoy nature. Recent surveys show how difficult it is to find a tranquil area. Shopping centres are increasingly situated in the country and many new roads are under construction in green areas. Ultimately, elitism as a charge should be brought against developers, not environmentalists.

What then is the role of the artist in any changes we might make to Norbury Park? What aesthetic should be created for Norbury Park in the twenty first century? The word 'aesthetic' is likely to make one think of art and fear that Norbury Park will be transformed into an open air gallery, a setting or backdrop for art objects, thereby losing its character as wild nature. But the creative artist plays an integral part in our culture by adapting traditional values to new eras. I have been outlining some traditional values and traditional beliefs about value which, I have claimed, show signs of going through a phase of decline rather than adaptation. With a new millennium approaching, my hope would be that artists would seek to revitalise what is good in our tradition.

Art in this century has sought the new, the shocking. It has been more concerned with itself than with nature. Yet even in this century, some artists have sought to recreate in their work the experience of simply being in nature. Such work springs from and seeks to communicate aesthetic appreciation which is not primarily of art, but of nature. The art work aspires to produce experiences of awe, wonder, tranquillity most properly occasioned by nature itself. The natural world, because it is our natural home, is too easily taken for granted. We take for granted the privilege of having such a home which delights as well as sustains, the fact that the world makes sense to us perceptually and not just conceptually, that our bodies and our senses are attuned to it and that we perceive it as ordered, predictable, harmonious, and beautiful. Art can remind us of these things and open up our senses to nature. But no art or artifact can replace nature because artifacts have human makers with human purposes. Nature, in contrast, is essentially not of our making; it is other and its otherness is precisely what we wonder at and would feel a profound and distinct sense of loss if it went.

Sunflower seed head

This is not to say that we should leave nature alone, leave Norbury Park to its own devices. It might seem that, in claiming more than instrumental value for nature, and in speaking of nature as 'unspoilt' or 'wild', I would wish to claim that wild nature has an intrinsic value and that Norbury Park should be permitted to become wilder than it currently is. For all manner of reasons, that is surely impractical. It would not be in keeping with the history of the park. Nor would it serve to improve our interactions with nature, since it would involve drastically curbing those interactions. But our interactions need to be respectful of the otherness of nature, guided by deep sensitivity to nature as our home. Some changes we make to nature tread the fine line between enhancing and despoiling, between developing nature's own aesthetic potential and imposing a design on it which might have the effect of incorporating it into the world of art and artifact. If Norbury Park is to be changed, let it be a change which reveals rather than conceals the wild, natural character of the park. If the change is to be directed by an artist, let it be an artist who has a proper sensitivity to nature and especially to its otherness.

The kind of appreciation of nature I have described both stimulates and can be enhanced by greater knowledge of nature. We need to develop our own potential as well as nature's. What is needed to deepen aesthetic appreciation is not, or not merely, theoretical knowledge, but the ability to recognise, to discriminate and to read nature. We cannot appreciate the beauty of what we do not notice. Often, in nature, one does not experience what is there because one does not know what to look, listen or sniff for. A geologist, botanist, ornithologist has skills of detecting, recognising, and reading which can make their experiences of nature and its beauties richer. The labelling, naming, classifying can be irritating at first, distracting from the experience. But once the theoretical knowledge becomes 'second nature', once one incorporates the knowledge into one's experiential repertoire, one has a greater openness to what nature has to offer to the senses.

Other kinds of knowledge can aid our appreciation of nature in a similar way. Knowledge of the history of a place such as Norbury Park, how past generations have affected and been affected by it can stimulate the historical imagination and provide a richer reading of the place. Knowledge of the arts, how painters, poets, composers have been inspired by nature and what they have found in it, can open one's senses to what is there.

New centuries, and, more so, new millennia are times to celebrate. Artists might look for features of modern life to celebrate and use their creative and communicative powers to integrate what is good in the traditional with what is best in the new. From our tradition, we have a seriousness about values which has recently declined and is in need of restoration. We have a need for knowledge and sensitivity about what we value. Concerning the aesthetic value of nature, we have our primordial contact with nature and our sensory appreciation of it as our home. All these are worthwhile features of our tradition, worthy to be adapted for the present age. What in this present age is there to celebrate? The obvious candidates are science and technology.

opposite. Cells of the lens of the eye

This century is seeing vast and amazing advances in both of these areas. For present purposes I would single out specifically ecological science and information technology. Artists with a deep appreciation of nature and a desire to express and to communicate it to others should learn about both. They could use their creativity to interpret what ecology has to offer and communicate with the help of information technology. If this task is left to the scientists and the technologists, the spectre looms of classrooms, equations, computer screens and virtual reality machines, all resulting in no greater appreciation whatever of actual nature. That is why the artist has a vital interpretative and creative role.

In recent years, our understanding of how the natural world works has increased enormously. We still by no means know everything; but we do know that there is a lot we do not know. Nature is quite extraordinarily complex. How to interpret the findings of ecological science, what conclusions to draw about the natural world from the support it gives for chaos theory and complexity theory are contentious issues. Some believe, however, that scientific evidence points to the need for a radically new model of nature. The old model is one of mechanism made up of isolatable parts or atoms which obey universal laws and are therefore, in principle, essentially predictable. New models being explored are nature as organism or community rather than mechanism, creating, evolving, developing parts in keeping with the whole, unpredictable even in principle. The natural world is not just so complex that collecting the data necessary for prediction defeats even our sophisticated computers; it is complex in an entirely different way: new forms of life emerge and old ones disappear which no amount of evidence could have enabled us to predict, for no previous state of the world determined or made inevitable, these occurrences.

Ecological science tells us that relations between animals or plants and their habitats are not simply relations of mutual use between separate individuals, but are 'symbiotic': parts of nature depend on each other not just for sustenance but for their fundamental characters: they are as they are because of where they are. Habitats are as they are because of their inhabitants and the inhabitants are as they are because of their habitats, so one cannot hope to understand one without the other. These relations it is claimed are best understood not on mechanistic models but on some more holistic model. Such conceptions, albeit still in their infancy, are fascinating, and very much to be explored, developed, better understood in the twenty-first century. Unfortunately, the 'our' in 'our understanding' refers to a few scientific ecologists. Many visitors to Norbury Park probably know quite little about what it is they are experiencing, how robust or fragile the ecosystem is, how the species got there, how species interact with each other and with their habitats, how the whole thing works. The findings of science are themselves something to celebrate for the millennium; knowledge of these findings will transform and enhance appreciation of nature. We need not only to acquire that scientific knowledge, but to apply it, to develop skills of recognising habitats and bird calls, reading rock formations, finding clues and interpreting them into an account of why the place is as it is.

If we are going to respect, value and protect Norbury Park, we had better find out what we have there. I am not suggesting scientists can tell us the whole story, far from it; even less that they can tell us what ought to be done, that is not their province; but they do have a story, though it is one which perhaps the scientifically knowledgeable creative artist, the communicator, the writer rather than the scientist is best equipped to tell.

Ecology or natural history is by no means the only history of Norbury Park. It also has a rich social history. This historical knowledge can also transform experience: there is a Druid's grove, but what do visitors actually know about the Druids? What do they know about Norbury Park's imports and exports, about its relations, past, present, and future, with the rest of the world? Having that knowledge can add an entirely new dimension to the experience of the Park. The historically knowledgeable artist might again be the person to stimulate historical interest.

Present activities in Norbury Park are similarly not without interest. Since 1931 it has been minimally managed, but it is managed and this is something which interests people and enriches their experience. The nineteenth century Danish philosopher, Kierkegaard, wrote (possibly tongue in cheek, but not without relevance today), that the prime human motivation is not the pursuit of pleasure, but the avoidance of boredom. Could this be why leisure can be a problem, why a favourite leisure pursuit is watching others at work? Think of fishing ports, cathedrals, even building sites. They seize our interest, stimulate imagination. We ask questions, and when we get the answers, this enhances our interest and our appreciation of the place. If work, farming or forestry, is to go on in Norbury Park, make it interesting to watch. While people are watching they are learning and thinking and noticing and, with luck, they are not trampling on rare species. There is a sawmill. Where does the wood go? What is it used for? How does the mill work? Answers to such questions, if given creatively, stimulate the imagination, deepen the appreciation.

There are three areas then, work, history and science, where knowledge of Norbury Park could enhance appreciation of it. But how are we to get that knowledge across? I have suggested that artists, creative communicators, might have a role. They might seek to let nature show itself and enable people to read what it shows. How exactly the artist is to fulfil this role is for the artist to determine: the results of the creative process are, of their nature, unpredictable. I do, though, have some general guidelines, a broad brief for the artist. There are

Geraint Cunnick, *Storytelling and Allegory,* Druid's Grove, Norbury Park

two problems: one from the point of view of the park; the other from the point of view of the people. Take the park first. The artist's job is to make the park legible, to make it tell its own story, seizing interest, inviting the imagination to project onto it, so that the knowledge can transform the experience. But nature must not be festooned with labels and information boards, transformed into a cultural artifact with human footprints everywhere. The otherness of nature must be preserved because that is what is of value, that is what a deep appreciation of nature is. The problem with respect to people is how to inform them in a way which stimulates imagination and engagement with the park. That is a further reason against information boards: they do not do that. It is one thing to have the knowledge; quite another to use the knowledge to read nature. Information boards all too often ruin the experience of nature, and they rarely work. People rarely take in the information or, if they do, they do not feed it back into the experience. Could that be why they are prone to being vandalised?

This is surely a problem which we can use information technology to address. We could use information technology somehow to lead people to a deeper understanding and appreciation of nature in general and Norbury Park in particular! But it must be done with sensitivity to both nature and people. People must not be bombarded with facts, but encouraged to ask questions. Anything they learn about nature, they must learn to recognise in nature, so that the knowledge transforms their experience rather than becoming a substitute for it.

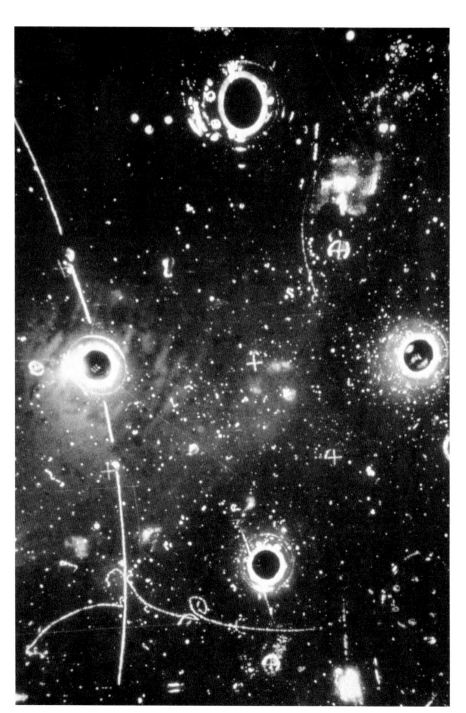

A Lepton event

Technology is to be celebrated, but only if it is properly used. It should be our servant not our master. If we become like machines, we risk being taken over by them. And we are becoming more like machines: constantly having to adapt our habits to their capacities. Our children have amazing and admirable facility with machines, but they have to be taught to play with each other.

Historians and scientists are not necessarily the best people at communicating what they know or stimulating the imagination in that way; or if they are, it is because they are wearing a different hat. We do not want or need learned tomes full of statistics and dates about social history, or scientific facts and figures and equations. Perhaps the literary rather than the visual artist would be the best candidate for giving the knowledge—a story-teller bringing the park to life with anecdotes. An area of the park was some time ago planted with walnut trees which were then sold to be used as rifle butts in a war in Europe. Knowing that, one's experience of the whole scene is immediately transformed. One is, via the park, continuous with a history and the place acquires a whole new atmosphere. Now that is just a brief anecdote with no historical detail; but enough to get the imagination working and to hold one's attention. We want artists as communicators to encapsulate the spirit of an age or place or ecosystem into anecdotes which are memorable and readable into the fabric of the park. Historians and scientists discover the facts, artists can communicate them in a digestible and stimulating way. But only, of course, if the artists take the trouble to find them out.

Finally, on natural beauty. It is perhaps for artists, not philosophers, to offer a vision of natural beauty. But it surely should not be a harking back to old images of the romantic or picturesque. The Enlightenment notion of aesthetic experience as detached, disinterested appreciation of pure form may no longer be relevant. What we want to do with forms is not gaze at them or translate them into static two dimensional representations. We want to hear them, feel them, taste and smell them, get to know them, feel a part of them instead of apart from them. That is how we might celebrate the primordial contact with nature of which we as humans are capable. We might even come to rediscover or reinterpret what Wordsworth meant when he wrote of nature as our moral educator. To be sure, we have outward bound training courses designed to build character and encourage teamwork; but my hunch is that Wordsworth would not have looked kindly on such an essentially instrumental use of nature. His insight was surely more to do with the moral sensitivity and strength which can develop from contemplating the strivings, the vast forces, the integrity, the harmonies in nature, and from coming to terms with our place in it. Aesthetic contemplation and moral education are perhaps not radically separate things. Perhaps it is both aesthetically and morally educative to come to realise that, whatever we do, however much we use technology to change the park, however many artifacts we introduce, given time, perhaps enough time for our human species to become extinct, but still, nature will recover, will cover up our works as the hill covers the railway which runs through Norbury Park.

In conclusion, we had better find something to celebrate in nature before it disappears. Norbury Park could be violated by insensitive use. It cannot accommodate vast hoards of tourists who would destroy what is of value there. But if those who go there are brought to be able to recognise what is there and to respect it accordingly, that would enhance its value. Value is not something we happen upon out there, like a park bench; nor is it something we produce and cast out into the world like old sweet papers; it is a relation which grows and develops to be nurtured and explored to reveal its multifaceted character. The exploration and enhancement of value can reveal all manner of richness in the valued object, the valuing subject and the complex relations between them. The Norbury Park project should be as much an educational one as a management one. The twenty first century, or anyway the beginning of it, might be an ambitious target!

George Barrett, *Scene in Norbury Park,* circa1780

Cornering around
Right of Way

Eileen  White

Wayfarers Walk, Hampshire

The practice of landscape design in public spaces requires an explicit social aesthetic. Now. How we meet one another, pass on a path, track or road, or occupy a picnic site or car park, is never just 'natural'. Skilled performance is needed to take into account one another's presence, without being obtrusive, offensive, or threatening. Managed landscape shapes the way we see one another: those who are familiar and those who are strangers. Its design constrains or eases contact among people.

As a metaphor which is often read into the landscape 'Arcadia' offers a comforting view of open green space. It avoids characterisation of the present and future. It represents the social world as peopled by familiars who are hierarchically ordered through an agreed understanding of mutual interdependence. It highlights a connectedness of kin, little social or geographical mobility, an overlap between place of residence and place of work, a local economic self-sufficiency, and a long historical sweep. Change is slow and understood as organic growth.

Arcadian imagery harkens back to the imagined comfort of a slow-moving society. Slow-moving societies have common values, rules and conventions about sharing space. These are typically sanctioned by religion drenched in aesthetic resources. Initiation into a slow-moving society equips us from birth with stories, music, dance, which tell us how to share space. A slow-moving society occupies a territory and its members feel part of a community. Identity derives from rootedness to a place rather than simultaneous commitment to multiple places or to movement between places. To be banished from such a society is a devastating punishment. The comfort may be deeply oppressive, but people know who they are and where they stand.

Fast-moving societies threaten the notion of Arcadia. By contrast they have blurred and clashing values, rules, and conventions. We may feel as if we are hovering on the brink of a future in which settled identity is disrupted. Our skills in knowing how to share public space are at risk. There may be no 'us' to whom public space belongs. Our sharing of space may come to be dominated by privately owned places such as the mall and the theme park. Access may come to be licensed by the smart card, the DNA fingerprint, the ability to pay. There are temptations to hide from the future in which we are creatures of the car, mobile phone, internet and virtual reality. Places don't stay put: a Eurostar advertisement on the railway line from London to Leatherhead and Dorking tells us that Ashford in Kent is a suburb of Paris and Brussels. As the ground shifts beneath us it may be difficult to discern common ground thus engendering a fear of social diversity.

If the old Arcadia was about an idyllic given community, a new Arcadia requires determined commitment to make it possible for people who do not know one another to interact in potentially dangerous spaces. The landscape could promote our ability to see ourselves as connected to one another and to nature. It could retrieve the notion of community from Arcady while stripping it of its sentimentality. This is partly an aesthetic challenge, but it is also partly a challenge to face up to the inequality that exists within access to public space. Management of space can proceed without worrying about the metaphors we use. It can proceed with ad hoc admission of new categories of user without being explicit about who else is being excluded and why. In attempting to be more socially inclusive, we will need to invent what I call 'rites of way'.

There is considerable evidence that access to green space may benefit our physical and mental health and my initial concern in considering Norbury Park was with questions of access for local people to health promoting environments. This prompted me to stumble on further questions of how people from different social worlds can share space and how the health needs of the population could feed into identifying and resolving the design problems of such.

## Arcadian Norbury

Norbury Park rises dramatically from the Mole Valley in Surrey with Leatherhead to the north and Dorking to the south. Arcadian metaphor does not engage the existence of the M25 or A24, the concept of the suburb, nor the fact that many Surrey residents work in the service sector of a world city. It does not engage the stretching of psychological boundaries as the South East comes to realise that it is a European region. The environs of Norbury Park are solidly within what was, until the 1980s, known as the Outer Metropolitan Area; an area which spilled over from London from the 1950s gaining more that a million inhabitants in the twenty five years from 1960. Surrey is now said to be in ROSE: the Rest of the South East excluding London. This part of England has been decisively shaped by modern transport technology; in the nineteenth century by railways and in the twentieth century by car. It has a busy intercontinental airport near the county boundary. Visitors to Arcadian Norbury Park are never out of earshot of motorway and aeroplane noise.

The park is zealously protected by local people who express concern about the threat of crass theme park development and depredation from London day-trippers. My visits to the park had made me wonder whether the poorly signposted park was deliberately hidden. Perhaps it is being protected from would-be visitors, including local people, who do not fit into the Arcadian imagery held so dearly by its most vocal defenders.

There is much hankering after Arcadian life in Surrey, but the Mickleham Parish Magazine gives us a glimpse of the complexity of the fast world that local people experience. They take pride in having saved the village shop and post office through a co-operative investment amongst local people. At the same time they worry about the threat of the coming of Burger King, a golf course, and the "desecration of an SSSI (Site of Special Scientific Interest) at Juniper Hill without planning consent". On the doorstep of Norbury Park, the varied messages at the entrance to the Leatherhead Leisure Centre demonstrate the confusing pace of change in the area. A plaque on the wall from its founding in 1974 tells us that the centre is for all local residents. The more recently installed neon sign spells *bienvenue* and *willkomen*.

In fact Norbury Park, Surrey and ROSE are full of strangers. The present owners of Norbury Park House, British for two generations and living there year round, contrast with the owners of other imposing residences, the latter being foreign businessmen who fly in. In the midst of Norbury Park are more strangers. It is home to the Bothy where the "country's largest practical conservation charity" trains, leads, and equips "50,000 active volunteers to carry out vital conservation work" ranging from "protection of wildlife habitats to the improvement of access to the countryside". Owned by Surrey County Council, the Bothy hosted in 1966 "groups from Germany and Turkey... involved in projects around Surrey such as bridge building and woodland management".[1]

Underpass: A24

Upmarket, respectable strangers have their place in and around Norbury Park, but there could be an easy slide from respectability. The graffiti in the grim underpass, crossing from Box Hill to the Norbury Park side of the A24 would not look out of place in the environs of Kings Cross. Smack on the doorstep of the good folk of Mickleham, in a car park on the A24, is the meeting place for the motorcycling fraternity who congregate in their hundreds from across the South East to celebrate their passion for a visual and sound culture of their own. The fear of contact which spills over into a fear of crime is coming to be recognised as a public health issue. The fear of contact is no longer confined to urban areas (if it ever was), but part of everyone's experience of public space.

Any attempt to make the park's existence more visible and accessible will make it more accessible to strangers whose cachet as 'respectable' may not be assured. This will make contact in the park less predictable for those who presently use it, not least for older women walking their dogs. But a land management strategy for public open space should take into account the health needs of the local population, many sections of which are presently excluded from the park.

**Towards a Healthier Life**

In discussions of inequality Surrey figures as an exemplar of wealth and health on the lucky side of the North/South divide. A wealthy county, it has some of the best health statistics nationally. If access to health promoting public green space is difficult here then there may be lessons for other affluent areas in ROSE and more broadly in the UK which has a comparatively poor record in respect of much preventable disease. Furthermore, since inequality in wealth damages the health status of all sections of the population and not just those who are poor, there are lessons for the whole of Britain which has the deepest inequalities in Western Europe.[2]

The major task of health promotion is to make it easier for people to live healthier lives. Large sections of the population take less physical exercise than they should and less than they think they should. But regular physical exercise has been identified as having multiple protective effects on health. Medical conditions which are widespread in the population are also major scourges in Surrey, impairing the quality of life and accounting for a large call on public services and private resources. Many health problems experienced by older people such as coronary heart disease and osteoporosis have long lead in times. A good start in life promotes health and prevents disease and disability at all ages. This applies to physical and mental health.[3]

The message about the economic benefits of prevention has not been lost on the private sector. Health insurers are sufficiently convinced that regular physical exercise prevents conditions which incur health care costs that lower private health insurance premiums are offered to subscribers who join health clubs.[4] This is of particular importance in affluent areas such as Surrey. It also serves to reinforce the separation between the economically stronger and weaker members of the population. Steps need to be taken to make it easier for all local people to engage in regular physical exercise. This is especially so with respect to less well-off residents. The picture that we are given of health in Surrey suggests that Norbury Park could be an outstanding resource for local people in adopting healthier lifestyles through regular physical activity.

## Access to Norbury Park

But how easy is it to get to Norbury Park? Life in Surrey is dominated by the car and other motorised vehicles and is becoming more so. 96% of visitors to Norbury Park arrive by car. This may be alright for the 40% of Surrey households which have two or more cars. But what does this mean for the 17% which have none? Since 1981 there has been a dramatic increase in travel to work by car, with reductions in travel by rail, bus, cycle and foot.[5] At the same time there is a big difference between men and women. Men are more likely to get to work driving a car or taking the train. Women travelling to work by car are likely to be passengers rather than drivers. 'High proportions' of women get to work as "car passengers, using the bus, cycling or on foot".[6]

British Rail developments have not made it easy for local people to get out and about either. The Surrey Environment News urges locals to come to Norbury Park by rail alighting at Box Hill & Westhumble Station. You get your tickets from the self-service machine at this now unstaffed station. The public lavatory in the station has been bricked in and access for the disabled to the northbound platform is long overgrown and locked. New occupants of the erstwhile ticket office, a congenial and public spirited cycle rental company, are keen to see facilities extended for disabled people, but so far have only been able to make access easier for the largely young male mountain bikers for whom paths through the park have been negotiated. Ad hoc co-operation with Surrey County Council has resulted in the production of the Norbury Park Family Off Road Cycle Route. Designation of the cycle path as a 'family' route is consistent with Arcadian imagery, despite its overwhelming use by young men. Making Norbury Park accessible by public transport and foot is crucial.

Westhumble and Box Hill Railway Station

## Preventable Conditions?

Coronary heart disease (CHD) is the commonest cause of death nationally. Despite a large improvement in the death rate from CHD in England and Wales (with 30% fewer premature deaths than a decade ago), twice as many men under 65 die than in comparable countries in Europe.[7] Directors of Public Health in Surrey have highlighted the problem of CHD and stroke and the need to counter these conditions with a programme to increase physical exercise backed by all local agencies. The local response includes a project begun in 1993 in which General Practitioners prescribe exercise in a leisure centre. But this is a response once damage is done. Primary prevention is treated as essential to the strategy. This means encouraging all sections of the population to include physical exercise as a regular feature of their daily lives.

As people live longer, their extra years of life also include disability. Most cost is expended on us when we are older. We can slow down the rate of increase in disability and the resulting rate of increase in call on services and their costs. With more costs for community care becoming means-tested following the 1990 NHS and Community Care Act, many services which were previously free at the point of use have to be paid for to local authorities out of personal savings. While the public sector is concerned to compress morbidity to save money, the most important reason for individuals to compress their own morbidity is to improve their quality of life as well as that of family and friends who might otherwise be called on to act as informal carers. Fries argues that regular physical activity is a strong candidate as the key variable for compressing morbidity in older people, via extending the period of disease-free and disability-free life expectancy. Elimination of non-fatal disabling diseases, such as osteoporosis, results in absolute compression of disability free life expectancy.[8]

Opening access to unwalkable footpaths on the Gower Peninsula

Britain has a large proportion of its population over retirement age. 16% of the population are elderly. This is expected to rise to almost one quarter of the population by the year 2030. With significant proportions of older people living on their own, it is particularly important to ensure that they maintain physical and mental fitness. Osteoporosis, which is implicated in hip and other bone fractures, occurs most frequently in women and increases with age. Regular weight-bearing exercise, such as walking, helps to build strong bones in children and young people and prevent the loss of bone density in older people, especially women after menopause. There is evidence that people, especially young women are less physically active than in the past.

Although statistics on the extent of disability in Surrey are not available, Surrey Social Services estimate that a significant number of elderly people suffer from some form of disability.[9] Evidently, such individuals place different demands on Norbury Park. For such individuals to benefit from Norbury Park, different design needs have to be met. Since the eighteenth century priority has been accorded to the visual mode in the aesthetic of Norbury Park. Hence, landscape management has attended to 'views'. In the past, visual considerations ensured that a railway within the park was hidden in a tunnel below its land.

But what importance is accorded to other sensory modalities? Since 1779 Leatherhead has been home to the Royal Society of the Blind, now known as SeeAbility. It provides supported housing for more than one hundred residents aged between 18-90 years old who have visual and other impairments, such as learning difficulties. Residents visit the Royal Horticultural Gardens at Wisley which have wheelchair access and specially scented areas designed for those with visual impairments. Its active environmental awareness group has been tape-recording woodland sounds and designing a nature trail. The East Surrey Learning Disability and Mental Health Services Trust runs a sheltered workshop in which participants design and build furniture for disabled clients. The rights of way team carry out improvements to public footpaths and bridleways. In Norbury Park there is a need for gates, pathways, furniture, toilets and stiles designed for disabled users, as well as information and transport which make regular visits an ordinary and easy occurrence. Access for people with disabilities should be designed and informed by the advice of the Countryside Commission. Their checklist should be the starting point for discussion with local disabled people.

As Richard Mabey suggests elsewhere in this collection, participation should not just be about decision making: it could be about local people working together in the park. In my view this would be a good start, especially if it drew participants from all social groups of all abilities including those in non-car owning households and children. All of those who are potential visitors are potential contributors to nurturing Norbury Park.

**A Social and Aesthetic 'Rites of Way'**

This is at bottom a matter of inventing new methods of democracy in which local people work with artists on design problems. Artists should be partners in inventing what I call 'rites of way'. The help of artists is crucial to achieve design standards that make social inclusion appear effortless. They can help us to re-imagine our most deep-rooted tendencies as social beings who need public green space.

Exponents of the new socio-biology assert the universality of the human species as an underpinning for aesthetic judgement. The physicist John Barrow notes that it has been "fashionable since the 1960s to regard all interesting human attributes as... learned from our contacts with individuals and society".[10] This makes strangers into enemies to one another with no foundation for aesthetic or moral judgement. In contrast with this fashionable position many scientists point to a common heritage that infuses our bodies and minds. As Barrow asserts "We have instincts and propensities that bear subtle testimony to the universalities of our own environment, and that of our distant ancestors".

We are primed to live in an old, dark, large, cold universe in which our species has adapted to more than two million years of hunting and gathering in tropical savannah habitats. Aesthetic responses regarding social interaction and nature derive from adaptations for safety and survival in such habitats. It is not an accident that we are attracted to landscapes which allow furtive observation from a place of safety: this allows exploration of potentially risky terrain which may yet offer sources of food and other resources. Barrow argues that artists know how to tap into and heighten an emotional awareness of features of our shared legacy, modified by our long history as hunter-gatherers. Artists can grasp aspects of the world and aspects of our nervous system well before they are described and explained by scientists. The best known example of this is artists' use of perspective. In plumbing what is most salient to us emotionally artists have been able to capture our deepest response to landscape. Landscape can be managed to help us rediscover our common legacy, as Jay Appleton argues elsewhere in this collection.

In celebrating our eternal essence, however, artists also explore the boundaries and edges of our feelings and tendencies. In so doing, they regularly trespass and expose possibilities to us. This is of profound cultural significance because although some of our propensities "... are... unalterable... others can be partly overwritten or totally reprogrammed".[11] In the smallest recent flash the overwriting has hurtled us from a vast history as hunter-gatherers, through rapid experiences of settled agriculture to commercial society, into a social form based on global economic and information flows. We need to be able to hold simultaneously our universal emotional rootedness as sometime hunter-gatherers in this universe (the basis for transcultural intersubjectivity) and the cultural flexibility reflected in our history of overriding what is given (the basis for babel and innovation).

Aesthetic intervention in landscape practice in fast-moving societies can, however, cope with conflict, confusion, and anxiety about who is linked to whom and how, and who has access to which spaces, through a number of gambits. It can exclude all but formal relationships. This licenses the artist to suspend a characterisation of the social by excluding the human presence altogether. It can focus on biological relationships amongst species of flora and fauna. In so doing an ecological agenda can be formulated which treats the biological as separate from human activity. It can highlight the past encapsulated from the present. It can emphasise one sensory modality informing emotional experience, such as vision, while ignoring others. Each of these gambits allows abdication of responsibility in the distribution of power in how space is currently used.

But as a branch of philosophy about how we relate to one another and to nature, aesthetics is nowhere more plausible than in practices shaping the spatial configuration of human contact. It is most important where contact amongst strangers is possible. This applies to town planning, architecture and landscape. The landscape can be a multi-sensory stage which helps us to imagine what we are and shape what we make of ourselves. Landscape design need not resort to sentimental metaphors. It should not be based on an unanalysed defence of space to sustain unequal relationships.

## From Arcadian Conservation to Social Diversity

Norbury Park has undergone a transformation from local self-sufficiency to regional and international interdependence. There is a hidden history here: three farms formed an interconnected agrarian system linked to a self-sufficient local economy organised by and for the park, whose household is said to have comprised three hundred people. This period of the park's history provides the closest approximation to the Arcadian picture.

Arcadian metaphor dominates the present aesthetic practice at Norbury Park. Arcadian preoccupation is clear in the operation and self-representation of Bockett's farm, one of three original farms on the estate. Documentation on the provenance of the farm traces it to the gift of a twelfth-century Norman baron to his man at arms, with a further area of land granted by the Lord of the Manor of Thorncroft and to the man at arm's thirteenth-century descendant, John de Leatherhead. The 'work' of Bockett's farm today includes the box-office 'take' which enables denizens of suburbs to experience a constructed rural past and feeds their identity by bypassing the present. A stone's throw from the paid attractions where children and animals are brought together in the presence of technology no more advanced than the pitchfork, the 'real' farmwork proceeds out of view, with sheep rounded up by tractor.

The transformation of the elements of Norbury Park from its past mode of production and form of life to the present could support exploration of links between aesthetic culture, social and natural ecology, personal and social identity, and economy. An understanding of the transformation of the three interconnected farms with the park's household of staff could support exploration of the catchments which now hold for production and consumption. This could prompt examination of the idea central to Agenda 21—sustainable development—in a more robust historical context than is usual.

The ecological imagination shining through Surrey County Council's Agenda 21 fits with the Arcadian metaphor. It is about conservation and restoration. Tantalisingly, a few of the events organised by rangers of the County Council present what could be central to a social function of public space, the exploration of ecological conundrums.

From the time of William Locke in the eighteenth century, Surrey residents were deeply implicated in the global activities centred in the world city of London. The exploration of ecological conundrums could locate conservation and management of biodiversity within the context of understanding the historical development of forms of life and work in Norbury Park and its environs. This exploration would not be confined to biodiversity, the touchstone of environmental agendas. It should take conundrums around our social diversity as central with the invention of 'rites of way' so that Norbury Park can be common ground for all.

## Notes

1   "British Trust for Conservation Volunteers in Mickleham", *Mickleham Parish Magazine*, 1966.

2   Wilkinson, R, *Unhealthy Societies: The Afflictions of Inequality*, London: Routledge, 1996. R. Wilkinson has argued that the deep economic inequalities which prevail in Britain lower health status through psycho-social mechanisms which reflect a fragile social fabric.

3   Glenister, D, "Exercise and Mental Health: A Review", *Journal of the Royal Society of Health*, February 1996, pp. 7-13. While serious mental illness especially that resulting in suicide is the preoccupation of much health promotion, mental health morbidity is widespread nationally. 20% of those consulting general practitioners present depressive symptoms, 25% of which are severe. Very little rigorous research has been conducted on the impact of exercise on mental health especially in the UK. Glenister's review of randomised control trials on the impact of regular physical exercise on mental health status finds encouraging evidence of effectiveness.

4   *The Times*, 26 April 1996, p. 29.

5   *Census Data Analysis: Workplace and Transport to Work in Surrey*, Surrey County Council Highways and Transport Department, 1996.

6   *Census* p. 13. This pattern although more sustainable is not attributed to environmental awareness but to the "prevalence of part-time/temporary work and corresponding low wage levels/short travelling distances". Hillman's (1993) research on the reduction in children's unaccompanied walking and cycling shows cuts in opportunities for regular physical exercise and the development of autonomy. The Director of Public Health for Mid-Surrey (1994) considered the implications of the pattern of car ownership to have worrying implications for the health of people in Surrey. Citing with approval an important study by the Public Health Alliance, he points out the way lack of car ownership is an indicator of deprivation in less urban areas where car ownership is crucial for access to essential aspects of ordinary life which benefit health including social support networks and the countryside. He concludes that: "Both the health promoting and health damaging effects of transport are unequally distributed in society. The people who experience the least benefit and the most disbenefit are those who are disadvantaged in many other ways. They include women, children, old people, the disabled, those on low income, and those who belong to a disadvantaged ethnic minority". *Improving the Health of Local People in Mid-Surrey: 1993/4*, Report of the Director of Health for Mid-Surrey, 1994, p. 18.

7   *Dear to our hearts: commissioning services for the prevention and treatment of coronary heart disease*, London: Audit Commission, 1996.

8   Fries, J. F., "Physical Activity, the Compression of Morbidity, and the Health of the Elderly", *Journal of the Royal Society of Medicine*, Vol. 89, No. 2, February 1996, pp. 64-68.

9   Nusselder, W. J., "The Elimination of Selected Chronic Disease in a Population. The Compression and Expansion of Morbidity", Washington D.C: *American Journal of Public Health*, Vol. 86, No. 2, February 1996, pp. 187-194.

10  "East Surrey Learning Disability & Mental Health Services", *NHS Trust Annual Report*, 1994-95.

11  Barrow, J., *The Artful Universe*, Oxford: Oxford University Press, 1995, pp. 91-113.

12  Barrow, *Artful*.

*A step into the shade, we find ourselves*
*in ramsons and hart's tongue ferns,*

*the faintly suspect pink*
*of campion,*

*ground ivy fledging the fence lines*
*with serpent blues,*

*bone-white arums,*
*hound's tongue, orchids,*

*docks. Seg leaves smell of meat,*
*the seeds are blood,*

*but call them gladdons: bring a wreath inside*
*at Corpus Christi; hang a small bouquet*

*of irises behind the kitchen door;*
*keep danger out with rabbit bones and hair,*

*with good intent, the last warmth of our kin,*
*the quiet ghosts who wander in the dusk,*

*unfolding the fernleaves,*
*revealing the yellow archangel.*

# *Wild Flower*

Six Norbury Park Dreamings
John Burnside

# Norbury Park—
# 65 Years Old

John Workman

In 1931, in the depths of the depression, Surrey County Council bravely intervened in the outstanding valley in which Norbury Park stands to prevent a rash of development staring out at Box Hill. After the war the County Council followed the national demands for increased production and more intensive use of land by developing forestry and farming, while at the same time allowing access whenever possible. At this time, a high percentage of parks were ploughed up, enclosed, afforested; many, of course, had the remains of wartime army camps, aerodromes and hospitals. No useful use was a luxury which few could indulge. Even parks like Petworth had herds of cattle and much supplementary feeding to add to the deer. Some later became country parks, theme parks, zoos, or even more intensive leisure facilities.

previous page. Rievaulx Abbey from Rievaulx Terraces

William Gilpin, *View into a winding valley* circa 1790

Corporate bodies may find it difficult to make decisions in an aesthetic field. The National Trust has difficulty enough, though it has limited objectives clearly set out. Whether to restore a park to Brown or Repton and remove all planting done in the last hundred years is difficult to decide. A County Council has changing councillors with differing views, a large staff with their own professional opinions, a vocal public with every conceivable and inconceivable opinion, and all the countryside agencies interfering with its own priorities and listings. Some offer grants to do positive things, others impose constraints to prevent the owner implementing new plans, however sensible. The Government too interferes with planning guidance, control of how money is spent, and capping.

In the 1960s my job was to repair parks, not restore them—certainly not to improve them. My objective was such that if you revisited a site in a thousand years the dominant appearance would be either Brown, Repton, Bridgeman or Kent. No trees would by then be original, but the style should be true to the creator and the species of the original concept only.

This year the National Trust produced an important document setting out its policies on the restoration and maintenance of historic landscape parks and gardens. This sets out all the factors to be taken into account before embarking on a restoration scheme, or indeed when making any management plan for an important landscape: historic precedent, archaeological evidence, the influence of landscape architects (famous or not), influences of the family, the relevance of age classes, and the possibilities for restructuring particular historic plants. The list is almost endless.

This paper is based on the National Trust's experience over the last forty years in managing and restoring well over a hundred historic landscape parks and gardens. The National Trust has the largest collection in the world of temperate plants, shrubs, and trees, stretching from Cornwall to Northumberland and from Kent to Northern Ireland, with all the variations of soil and climate, history, design and experience.

Everyone seems to agree that William Locke was a man of taste, greatly imbued with a love of landscape. Influenced by Gilpin he wanted something essentially picturesque, natural and romantic. The Payne Knight school rather than the Brown/Repton. No formality. Surprise views rather than vistas. No avenues. The peepholes of Rievaulx and Stourhead. Shady walks, variety of texture. There is a paper in this collection which refers to Locke being interested in statuary, but there is no mention of it in the grounds. There are seats, benches and platforms, but no buildings or temples. No water or watery surprises. The river is of no consequence. There is mention of new sweeping drives and the top of a hill being shaved off to improve a view. These might provide precedents for 'improvements' in the future.

The house is a very fine Italian villa, wonderfully placed, facing south, surrounded by a dream landscape. Groves, thickets, open spaces, trees of considerable but not great variety. The arboretum was, I would suggest, originally just the cedars and perhaps a very few other things to give effect to the approach. The house is now a hole in the original picture. I am reminded of Clumber Park, a huge area of 4,000 acres, a grand avenue three miles long and as you turn the final corner the enormous house is replaced by an ice cream kiosk.

I am, of course, a forester and proud of it. The plantings made at Norbury Park twenty, thirty, or forty years ago were, as far as I could see, a sensible choice of species, with sensible mixtures, mostly three-row, capable of developing into good broad-leaved woods. The fairly drastic interventions over the last few years are developing into rather open woodlands a bit prematurely, but successfully. The attractive open growth with widely spaced young broad-leaves should develop beautifully. The opening back to grassland in other areas is very attractive. The coppice areas are historic, interesting and good for conservation, though for me they are not particularly beautiful and I simply do not know how they relate to Locke's landscape. They were probably promoted during the Victorian era of management for shooting and not therefore of great significance.

Updown Wood was clearly a wood, but Fetcham Downs were probably more open and scrubby and rich in wild things. Foresters did terrible things thirty years ago—look at Hafod and Woodchester—so did architects and planners. Even Brown destroyed almost as much as he 'improved'. Even some conservationists exhibit tunnel vision and follow the flavour of the month. Dead trees are a current craze; a few years ago it was lichens or the retention of ivy. Too many of them are specialists in one particular field—birds, insects, fungi, flora—seldom is a holistic ecological approach adopted. I venture to suggest that a well-trained forester

Norbury Park House

should be the most able to get the whole picture right. He can, if he wishes or is told to listen to all the other expertise, sieve it and put a balanced programme into effect on the ground.

Most of my work with the National Trust and at home in the Cotswolds was directed to try to improve the beauty of the place over the centuries, but I was not ashamed to produce and sell timber as well. I have been able to demonstrate on dozens of properties that multiple objectives can be met. The wood at home was awarded The National Centre of Excellence in 1993. Not everything everywhere, but everything somewhere. There are conflicts, but they can be separated. I realise that I did not always get my priorities right; I did not, many years ago, have enough information. Now we can find out more of the history, more of the conservation value, more of the public's needs, to make better decisions. Some decisions are irreversible, some can be adjusted. Much damage was done in the past because some people were in too much of a hurry. If you tackle only 1% of the area in any year you can adjust your methods. If you start by doing 50% in 5 years, as too many

people did, you may have wrecked many of the true values and driven away the spirit of the place. In many respects, the rate of change is critical.

I am not considering the farmland in Norbury Park, though in the long term perhaps one should. Bockett's Farm has developed its own contribution. At Norbury Park the car parks are at the edges whereas at Box Hill they are in the middle, though you can walk over much of Box Hill and not meet a soul. I do not know how the public use Norbury Park; it is certainly not just a bit of ordinary countryside, nor is it a forest, a nature reserve, or a Stourhead. We should identify more of what it is that people who go there get out of it. People do now choose before they set out. The locals may just want air and exercise for themselves and their dog, but there must be those who come to Norbury Park for its own atmosphere rather than to Box Hill or Polesden Lacey or Ranmore or Chessington or Wisley. We should perhaps develop that particular experience rather than invent a new one.

I want infinite choice, but not all in one place. Norbury Park may have a secret character which I began to feel. One piece of sculpture was excellent—but I did not want a trail. At Brockhampton, however, I was impressed by a new sculpture trail, relevant to local history and folklore, done with the local schools which will clearly enthral the public in an otherwise fine, but relatively ordinary wood. We do not want the Teddy Bears' Picnic syndrome to get people in the wood at any cost.

At Norbury Park I wanted to see out more into the countryside, as did Messrs. Locke and Gilpin. I have developed quite a technique in cutting peepholes; inspired by the Rievaulx Terrace and Stourhead, you can, by cutting a few trees half way down a slope, open up an enchanting view of a building or natural feature without either damaging the skyline or producing a vista with inevitable scrubby foreground. You have to be brave but must cut timidly so that your view is precisely centred and pray that you do not have a gale for a couple of years.

Norbury Park has lost its heart, but we must give it a new spirit to give inspiration and pleasure. Forestry with its knowledge of how trees perform together has a part to play as well as arboriculture and all the other land based professions. A fusion of expertise will take time through a management plan, but it may still need an inspired person with some freedom to achieve the best result. Committees are not known for producing anything outstandingly aesthetic.

opposite. Box Hill

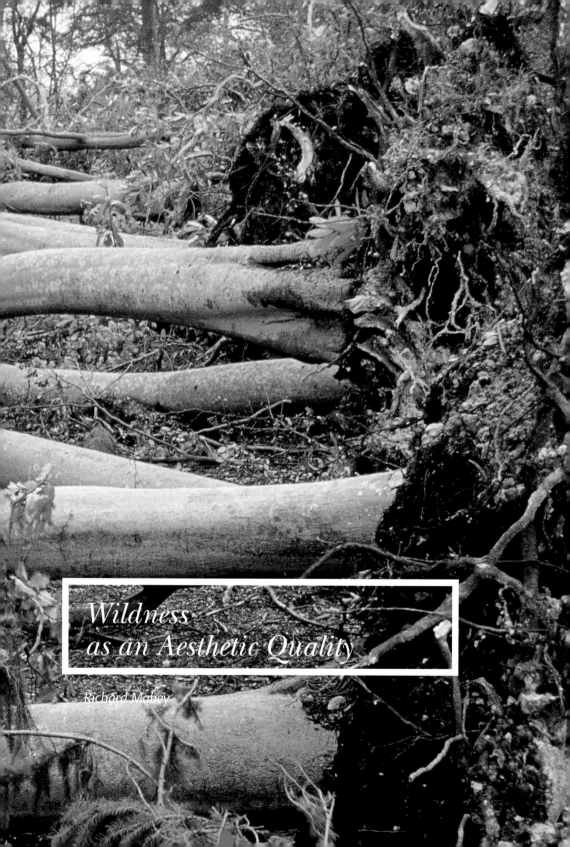

# Wildness
## as an Aesthetic Quality

Richard Mabey

Norbury Park

I chose 'wildness' rather than 'wilderness' as my theme since the idea of wilderness carries associations which are not really relevant in Britain, and certainly not in the English Home Counties. It suggests land beyond or before civilisation, which people may pass through, but do not stay or leave behind any significant imprint.

previous page. After the storm in October 1987, Sheffield Park, Sussex

Norbury Park is hardly that. I am not sure that much of it can even be described by that more vague and less stringent term 'wild'—meaning developing and growing according to its own designs. But I want to argue that the park might benefit precisely by moving in that direction, and to suggest that, far from needing more finely tuned management plans, what it needs is for us to back off.

It seems to me that if we are going to have a countryside that ordinary people enjoy, it must have qualities which contrast with those of the world from which they are escaping. It is hard to see what a park is for if it fails to deliver these. Certainly this has been the finding of several recent surveys on public attitudes towards leisure in the countryside. These have found that visitors are seeking experiences which are different from those in their workaday lives, where sense impressions are sharper, and where there is a sense of growth and renewal.

Derek Francis, *The Scrubs*, Norbury Park

But what visitors to the British countryside too often find is a landscape in which management is simply replicating the values of an industrial society dominated by business ethics and the market economy. It is ordered, analysed, interpreted; mown, clipped, weeded, planted-up and regimented. In many places managed to death. The idea that nature might have an autonomous life of its own to surprise and inspire us, and to teach us about limits, is something we seem to have forgotten, or maybe become fearful of. Even the institutions which run our increasingly over-managed countryside reflect the hierarchies of the business world, to the extent of borrowing its language. These days conservation bodies all have 'mission statements' and 'corporate goals'. They refer, depressingly, to the natural world as 'their product'.

Erddig, Clwyd

So I want to make out a case for the lessening of management and of the human appropriation of nature, not just at Norbury Park, but in the countryside as a whole. But I am not arguing for a removal or lessening of human presence, rather a lessening of planned, purposefully-directed management; for a certain style of human engagement, if you like, rather than a disengagement.

I also want to suggest that visual appreciation of the landscape is by no means the only kind, and that the conceptualisation of the landscape as an experience for the eye and our seemingly irresistible desire to turn nature into yet another human artefact are closely linked.

A common argument against reducing human interference in the landscape is that the countryside is already an almost wholly man-made artefact and that its continuity needs to be conserved. The contribution of an autonomous, vital nature inside the cultural framework is repeatedly underestimated in this model, as is the diversity of—and the frequent conflict between—the management goals and styles of different historical periods. Almost invariably one high-profile moment is subjectively chosen from a landscape's history and offered as the 'proper' or immemorial condition which conservation policies have to immortalise. In the case of Norbury Park it is the planned park landscape which was created for it in the eighteenth century.

Yet remains of Celtic field systems have been discovered at Norbury Park. Why have we ignored the Iron Age as a possible time frame? And the pre-Norman landscape? And the period when the park would have been cloaked with secondary woodland during the economic collapse and depopulation following the Black Death? Why do we instead choose a comparatively recent format, the country dweller's private park, which is not only one of the dullest options available, but also the most elitist? Parks were created so that rich people could have privileged views over the countryside and I am not convinced that it is the kind of model we should be referring to in the late twentieth century.

But first I would like to clear away one frequent but false misconception which is that to talk about 'wilderness' or 'wildness' is necessarily to invoke a model of an Arcadian past. The ecologist George Peterken has developed some useful concepts which can help make this retrospective reflex redundant.[1] He talks about 'past-naturalness' and 'future naturalness'. 'Past-naturalness' is that non-recreatable state of landscape before humans began to alter it. 'Future-naturalness' is what a landscape would become if humans took their hands off it now. For example, it is what a spruce plantation would aspire to if the Forestry Commission abandoned both the management and harvesting of it.

Derek Francis, *Trees and Storm Clouds*, Updown Wood, Norbury Park

Luton Hoo, Bedfordshire

The idea, however, that nature is our servant or plaything and that we should model or steward it according to our social and economic values, rather than respecting it as an alternative to them, does have its roots in the past, especially in the landscaping movement of the seventeenth and eighteenth centuries. It is a short move, in either direction, from the principle of enclosing a view of nature in a frame to the rearranging of the real thing so that it provides a pleasing vista from the 'Big House'.

Landscapers were quite open about the fact that they were 'taking possession' of nature. Tree planting, especially, combined what they regarded as estate beautification with a powerful symbolic statement about the planter's social status and its potential inheritance down through the generations—for as least as long as the life of a hardwood tree. Humphry Repton reckoned there was nothing that excelled it for those who wanted to display their territorial power and what he unashamedly described as the 'appropriation' of the landscape.

This determination to 'capture' nature (a term we still use to describe naturalistic paintings and photography), to freeze and hold it in an enclosure or framed view, is, of course, at odds with the way that natural systems actually work, but it has had a profound influence on the way we conceptualise natural systems. It has even affected the science of ecology and helped foster the idea of conserving discrete patches of natural landscape instead of the whole countryside. Until the great storms of 1987 and 1990, it also underpinned the notion that there might be such things as perpetually stable 'climax' tree communities in woodland!

An alternative way of regarding landscape (which Jane Howarth also refers to in this publication) is to regard them as narratives—dynamic, unfolding stories rather than static, albeit living, museum pieces. This catches both the vitality and unpredictability of succession in nature, and the way that ordinary people most often relate to nature and landscape. Amidst all the accounts of Norbury Park by great landscape engineers and writers I have been surprised that no one seems to have collected the memories and anecdotes of those who have lived near or simply used the park. John Berger in *Pig Earth* sees the function of storytelling as crucial to rural life: "this *gossip* which, in fact, is close, oral daily history, is to allow the whole village to define itself.... What distinguishes the life of a village is that it is also a living portrait of itself: a communal portrait, in that everybody is portrayed and everybody portrays".[2] Perhaps one of the objectives of those working at Norbury Park ought to be to re-engage with local gossip and story-telling.

I mentioned the great storm of 1987. This was unquestionably one of the most important events in the history of southern English landscape for the past three hundred years. It not only caused a huge disturbance to woods and individual trees, but to many people's assumptions about how woods 'work'. It began by bringing a great sense of loss to people, but ended, I think, by reinspiring them with an understanding of the resilience of living things, and of how woods are capable of renewing themselves.

Storm damage, Sheffield Park, East Sussex, 1987

Sadly, more damage than was ever done by the storm was wreaked by humans attempting to manage their way out of the problems it created. In some Sussex estates I saw bulldozers clearing away perfectly healthy groves of naturally regenerated beech and ash in order to make room for regimented rows of planted saplings. There is still, I am afraid, a widespread belief that trees are incapable of growing unless they are deliberately planted by humans, conveniently ignoring, in the process, most of the history of vegetation on the planet. It is as if self-sprung saplings do not qualify as real trees, but live in some kind of limbo between the natural and the man-made. One conservation agency that I will not name, issued a press release about the damage caused by the storm and made the same disjunction. "Trees", it announced, "are at great danger from nature". The organisers of a National Trust art exhibition also stated in their catalogue that the storm "had desecrated the past and betrayed the future".

Of course, it had done neither. It was a purely natural event that happens in England every few hundred years. And nearly a decade on, even those who were most affected and disheartened by its initial effects now acknowledge that it had an invigorating effect on the wooded landscape of the south. It reorganised even-aged and often monocultural plantations into more naturally varied stands. The great influx of light sparked off the most spectacular regeneration of young native trees that has probably been seen for half a century, and set the landscape on the move again. It took it out of the static frame of vista and into dynamic narrative. And not just into ecological narrative, but social narrative as well. Memories of the storm, of days trapped among fallen timber, of trees saved and neighbours rescued, of a camaraderie that reminded people of the Blitz, form one of the few common subjects in vernacular story-telling in the southern countryside.

I have friends in Suffolk who were trapped inside their house during the height of the storm, with the electricity and phone dead. They could see the trees round their house going down, but could not hear them because of the noise of the wind. Their Soay sheep had taken shelter close to the house and they could just glimpse their eyes glinting through the window. The Chilterns were less seriously hit than points further south, but I vividly remember the bizarre light conditions at the storm's height—an eerie green glow that was partly an atmospheric phenomenon, and partly a result of the air being full of flying vegetation; and what I thought were distant lightning flashes, were explosions caused by high voltage cables crashing down and shorting.

Wakehurst Place, West Sussex, 1987

Derek Francis, *Towards the Junipers*, Norbury Park

It was a cataclysmic event, but, as most people affected will admit, one of the most exciting in their lives, and that memory of an extraordinary night ought to be preserved in the landscape as well as in oral history. I was unsettled when I read the management plan for Norbury Park woods to see that for many of the compartments there was an intention and plan to "clear up storm damage". Perhaps it was for a more recent storm. But I would have thought that the conservation of remnants and echoes of such momentous natural events could be one of the ways that narratives of the place are kept alive in people's imaginations. In Green Park in London a few days after the storm, I saw one of the toppled plane trees being chain-sawed into a climbing frame by one of the park rangers. For children, needless to say, all of the fallen trees were a source of huge excitement. And for many naturalists—vertical orchid beds on the root-plates of upturned beech trees being one of the bizarre habitats which survived for a couple of years after the storm.

If I was looking for one example of how we might articulate our response to nature in a different way, it would be how we choose to remember, to talk about, to mythologise that storm: do we regard it as a malign event which is best swept under the woodland carpet, or as a catastrophe which alerted people to the power of nature and to the resilience of trees, and deserves to be commemorated?

Nothing of what I am saying about the regenerative powers of nature has anything to do with ignoring or excluding people. I am thinking more about the inappropriateness of certain attitudes towards nature, so that perhaps the model for human presence in Norbury Park is not that provided by landscape designers or conservation executives, but by the beaver—a creature that, like us, enjoys pottering in woods and doing a little imaginative landscape reconstruction, but never has the impertinence to say "I am in control". As human beavers, both the people looking after Norbury Park and those who are enjoying it might find a new kind of relationship with the natural world (and with each other) that has passed them by before because of our obstinate insistence on being in charge.

And why should these two groups of people not be the same? Why could the people who are regular visitors to Norbury Park not also be the ones who look after it—to the extent that it needs any looking after? Unless the people of Dorking and Leatherhead and the surrounding villages are dramatically different from the rest of the country, they would be able to help manage parts of Norbury Park as a community wood, to take part in the decision-making about its future, and to plan and lend a hand with the work. There are hundreds of such community woodland schemes now operating in Britain, many in urban areas, and they have been hugely successful both as ecological projects and community experiences.

Yet for such relatively unplanned, loose, egalitarian, low-intensity activity really to succeed in a large and heavily manicured site like Norbury Park, we would still have to confront our fears of wildness. Why are we so reluctant to let go of the reins? Do we still have the medieval's dread of nature? Do we feel guilty about what we have done to it? Or do we still truly believe that we know best? It is perhaps a bit glib to say that wildness is a condition of the mind as much as of the land. Yet it is true that wildness could be an aesthetic characteristic of many places and experiences—a "free fringed tangle at the edge of things" as the American writer Annie Dillard put it.[3] It does not have to involve grandiose or reckless adventures, gestures of derring-do. It can, in parks and gardens as much as in forests and on mountains, be a right we return to nature, to allow it room to move, to experiment, to enchant and to surprise us again. It is worth recalling that Wordsworth penned his famous line "a wilderness is rich with liberty" in a poem inspired by the release of two goldfish into a Lake District pool.[4]

Notes

1   See, for example, *Woodland Conservation and Management*, Chapman & Hall, 1981 and *Natural Woodland*, Cambridge: Cambridge University Press, 1996.

2   Berger, John, *Pig Earth*, London: Chatto & Windus, 1985, p. 9. First published by Writers & Readers Publishing Cooperative, 1979.

3   Dillard, Annie, *Pilgrim at Timber Creek*, London: Pan Books 1976.

4   Wordsworth, William, "Liberty" (1829), *Wordsworth Poetical Works*, ed. Thomas Hutchinson, Oxford: Oxford University Press, 1969.

opposite. Derek Francis, *Fallen Tree*, Norbury Park

*In the wheat-coloured shimmer of dusk, a dog-fox*
*crosses my path,*

*tracing his own*
*faint echo through the grass,*

*a glimmer of flesh, distilled from a lacing of smoke*
*and the dust of the sawmill*

                *Up on the hill, the old*
                *wartime searchlamp is gone,*

                *its beam of light*
                *still visible, in some far galaxy,*

                *though not the shape it traced*
                *against the trees,*

*and somewhere else the drone of homeward planes*
*still flickers in a stranger's instruments*

*as interference:*
*undecided noise.*

*Sometimes we pause, walking homeward, when we hear*
*the vixen's cry, the rabbit in the grass:*

*these living shapes go home into the dark,*
*where nothing ends, though we keep moving on,*

*and only a shadow remains*
*in the bushes and briars.*

# *Fox*

Six Norbury Park Dreamings
John Burnside

# Afterword

This publication is based on the conference *Arcadia Revisited: The Aesthetics of Land Management in the 21st Century* which took place in June 1996 at the Royal Geographical Society in London. Conceived and organised by Art Project Management, the conference was a response to Surrey County Council's decision to reconsider the future planning of Norbury Park, a 1,300 acre estate which lies between rural Surrey and Metropolitan London.

The Norbury Park project (funded by the Arts Council of England, South East Arts and Surrey County Council), highlighted the need, at the end of the twentieth century, for a formal debate between the visual arts constituency and those who are engaged in a contemporary analysis of, or are responsible for, the territories beyond towns. It also illustrated the artist's changing relation to the British landscape.

This combination of a visual arts events programme with a theoretical and academic study is an experimental device to educate and enthral all those with an interest in Norbury Park and similar sites, and one which we hope will establish a climate in which the contribution of artists to the management of landscape can be entertained.

The Norbury Park project which commenced in 1994 has employed artists, architects, landscape architects, a writer and a designer. The programme included artist residency schemes in the park and with neighbouring schools, a management masterplan, an artist led reminiscence project and a commission for the design of gates and seating. The aim was to create a holistic approach to the evolution of the park with a potential to solicit monies from the current National Lottery awards to assist towards that end.

By 1997 the project, funded in the main part by Arts Council of England and South East Arts with some support from Surrey County Council, was suspended while those responsible for the park considered a way forward. It is hoped that the aforementioned endeavours have supplied an enlightened context for the future of Norbury Park and similar much loved landscapes.

The artists involved in the project were:

| | | |
|---|---|---|
| Siah Armajani | Jonathan Cook | Tania Kovats |
| Walter Bailey | Geraint Cunnick | Kate Miller |
| Clare Barber | Claire Dalby | Claire Straiton |
| Birds Porchmouth Russum | Derek Francis | Stephen Turner |
| John Burnside | Steve Geliot | Richard Wentworth |
| Ashley Cartwright | Gillespies | Tommy Wolseley |
| Gary Clough | Uta Kögelsberger | |

# List of Illustrations

**Vicki Berger**

pp. 8/9. Aerial view of Norbury Park and environs

p. 11. Norbury Park, courtesy Surrey Record Office

p. 13. Norbury Park, courtesy Surrey Record Office

p. 14. Norbury Park, courtesy Surrey Record Office

**Richard Hoggart**

pp. 16/17. Norbury Park, 19th Century, courtesy Surrey Record Office

**Isabel Vasseur**

pp 30/31. David Nash, *Running Table*, Grizedale Forest, 1978, photo: Isabel Vasseur

p. 32. Christo and Jeanne-Claude, *Surrounded Islands*, Biscayne Bay, Greater Miami, Florida, 1980-1983

p. 33 top. Richard Long, *Dartmoor Circle*, 1992, courtesy of Anthony D'Offay Gallery, London

p. 33 bottom. James Turrell, *Roden Crater with Finished Bowl and Western Entrance*, 1985, courtesy of Anthony D'Offay Gallery, London

p. 34. Giuseppe Penone, *Otterlo Beech*, 1987-1988, Kröller-Müller Museum, Otterlo, The Netherlands, photo: Isabel Vasseur

p. 35. Tony Cragg, *Raleigh*, 1986, National Garden Festival, Gateshead 1990. Photo: Garden Festival staff photographer

p. 36. Constantin Brancusi, *Tirgu Jiu World War 1 Memorial Park, Roumania, The Endless Column*, 1935, courtesy of ET Archive

p. 37. Robert Smithson, *Spiral Jetty, Great Salt Lake, Utah*, 1970

p. 38. Andy Goldsworthy, *Sidewinder*, Grizedale Forest, 1984–5, photo: Isabel Vasseur

p. 39. Ian Hamilton-Finlay, Stockwood Park, Luton, 1986-1991, photo: Jane Heath

**Gillian Darley**

pp. 40/41. Water-meadows at Norbury Park, photo: Gillian Darley

p. 42. Painted room at Norbury Park House from sale particulars, 1916

p. 44. James Baker Pyne, *View of Avon from Durdham Down*, 1829, oil on canvas, City of Bristol Museum and Art Gallery, courtesy of The Bridgeman Art Library

p. 45. Sally Matthews, showing *Cows* on the Sustrans Cycle Route photo: Isabel Vasseur

p. 46. Viaduc des Arts, Paris, photo: Gillian Darley

p. 47. Georges Descombes, La Voie suisse, photo: Georges Descombes

p. 48 top. Christo and Jeanne-Claude, *Running Fence,* Sonoma and Marin Counties, California, 1972-1976

p. 48 bottom, p. 49. Geoffrey Jellicoe, John F. Kennedy Memorial, Runnymede, photo: Gillian Darley

p. 50. Memorial Garden, Montjuc, Spain, photo: Mary McHugh

p. 51. New French National Library, Tolbiac, Paris. photo: Gillian Darley

## Jay Appleton

pp. 56/57. View to Norbury Park House, photo: Derek Francis, 1995

p. 58. Norbury Park House, south side, from Norbury Park sales particulars 1930, courtesy Surrey Record Office

p. 59. Holman Hunt, *The Scapegoat*, oil on canvas, Lady Lever Art Gallery, Port Sunlight, Wirral, Courtesy of The Bridgeman Art Library

p. 60. Versailles, 1976 photo: Jay Appleton

p. 61. Claude Lorrain, *Landscape with Hagar and the Angel*, oil on canvas, courtesy of The National Gallery, London

p. 62 top. View of the park at Petworth House, West Sussex, designed by Capability Brown, photo: J. Whitaker, courtesy of The National Trust Photographic Library

p. 62 bottom. Beetling cliffs at Hawkstone, photo: Jay Appleton

p. 63. View from Norbury Park towards Box Hill, photo: Vicki Berger, 1994

p. 64. Farmland fringe, Norbury Park, photo: Vicki Berger, 1994

p. 66. Benjamin Pouncy after Thomas Hearne: An "Undressed Park" from Richard Payne Knight,*The Landscape: A Didactic Poem*, 1794, courtesy of Hereford and Worcester County Libraries

p. 67. Benjamin Pouncy after Thomas Hearne: A Park "dressed in the modern style" from Richard Payne Knight, *The Landscape: A Didactic Poem*, 1794, courtesy of Hereford and Worcester County Libraries

p. 71. Gateway to Norbury Park, from Norbury Park sales particulars, 1930, courtesy Surrey Record Office

p. 73. Fence, Norbury Park, photo: Vicki Berger, 1994

pp. 74/75. Edge of the wood, 1994, Norbury Park, photo: Vicki Berger

p. 76 top. Humphry Repton, drawing of Bayham Abbey, Kent, showing the landscape as it was, courtesy of Dorothy Stroud and Country Life Picture Library

p. 76 bottom. Humphry Repton, drawing of Bayham Abbey, Kent, showing the proposed improvements to the landscape, courtesy of Dorothy Stroud and Country Life Picture Library

p. 78. Humphry Repton, Longleat, Wiltshire, courtesy of Dorothy Stroud and Country Life Picture Library

## Richard Wentworth

p. 83. Teesdale

p. 87 top left. Dresden from the air

p. 87 top right. Munich from the air

p. 87 bottom left . Glasgow pavement

p. 87 bottom right. London pavement

p. 92. Frauenkirche, Dresden

p. 93. Chelsea Flower Show, 1996

## Tania Kovats

pp. 98/99. Tania Kovats, *Imports (Knickers)*, 1996

p. 100. *Gortex*, photo Tania Kovats, 1997

p. 101. Gortex advertisement— No Sweat, photo: Tania Kovats, 1997

p. 102. Camel Boots is a registered trademark of Worldwide Brands, Inc., photo: Tania Kovats, 1997

p. 103. Giotto, *St. Francis of Assisi Preaching to the Birds*, oil on canvas, Louvre, Paris, courtesy of Giraudon and The Bridgeman Art Library

p. 104–106 Stills from *The Evil Dead*, directed by Sam Raimi, 1980, courtesy of Renaissance Pictures

p. 107 top. Tania Kovats, *Grotto*

p. 107 bottom. Tania Kovats, *Landscape III: Cave*, 1995, courtesy of Lotta Hammer Gallery, London

p. 108 top. Tania Kovats, *Ledge*

p. 108 bottom left. Tania Kovats, *Landscape II: Tomb*, 1995

p. 108 bottom right. Tania Kovats, *Canyon*

p. 109 top. Tania Kovats, *Rocky Outcrop*

p. 109 bottom. Tania Kovats, *Rocky Outcrop*

p. 110 top. Tania Kovats, *Imports,(Glue Sniffing)*, 1996

p. 110 bottom. Tania Kovats, *Imports, (One Shoe)*, 1996

p. 111 top. Tania Kovats, *Imports (Pornography)*, 1996

p. 111 bottom. Tania Kovats, *Imports (Condom)*, 1996

p. 112. Gregory Crewdson, *Untitled* 1993/1994, courtesy of Jay Jopling, London

p. 113. Willie Doherty, *Blindspot*, Courtesy of Matt's Gallery, London

p. 114. Willie Doherty, *Barbaric Mire—Weeping*, courtesy of Matt's Gallery, London

p. 115. Graham Gussin, *Meeting (Number 1)*, 1991, courtesy of Lotta Hammer Gallery, London

## Ken Worpole

pp. 116/117. Phoenix Park, central London, 1994, photo: Ken Worpole

p. 123. Talbot Car, courtesy of Getty Images

p. 124. CCTV Cameras at Pallister Park, Middlesbrough, 1994, photo: Ken Worpole

p. 125. Leon Kossoff, *Children's Swimming Pool*, 1971, oil on board, courtesy of Tate Gallery Publications, London

p. 127. Girl Guides at Norbury Park, 1941, photo: Mr & Mrs Brookes, Fetcham, Surrey

p. 128. Coram's Fields, central London, 1994, photo: Ken Worpole

## Jane Howarth

pp. 136/137. Lead ion collisions produced by the experiment NA49, photo: CERN, Geneva

p. 138. Map showing railway line through Norbury Park, 1848, courtesy of Surrey Record Office

p. 143. Sunflower seed head, photo: George Bernard, courtesy of Science Photo Library

p. 145. Cells of the lens of the eye, photo: Professor P. Motta, courtesy of Science Photo Library

p. 149. Geraint Cunnick, *Storytelling and Allegory*, 1995, with pupils from St. Andrews School, Leatherhead in Druid's Grove, Norbury Park. photo: Geraint Cunnick

p. 150. A Lepton event—a neutrino interacting with an electron and emerging as a neutrino: first observation of "neutral currents" in the Gargamelle heavy liquid bubble chamber, photo: CERN, Geneva

p. 153. George Barrett, *Scene in Norbury Park*, c.1780, courtesy of Leatherhead and District Local History Society

## Eileen O'Keefe

pp. 154/155. Motorbikers' exhibition space: Rykers Car Park on A24 between Box Hill and Norbury Park, photo: Eileen O'Keefe

p. 156. Horse and cart: Wayfarers Walk, near Breach Farm, Hampshire, photo: Alan Howarth

p. 159. Underpass: A24 between Boxhill and Norbury Park, photo: John O'Keefe

p. 163. Westhumble and Boxhill Railway Station: bricked in lavatory, photo: John O'Keefe

p. 164. Opening access to unwalkable footpaths on the Gower Peninsula, from *South Wales Evening News*, reprinted in Rambling Today, Summer 1996

## John Workman

pp. 172/173. Rievaulx Abbey from Rievaulx Terraces, photo: Gillian Darley

p. 175. William Gilpin, *View into a winding valley*, c1790, courtesy of Leeds Museums and Galleries

p. 177. Norbury Park House, from sales particulars 1916

p. 178. Box Hill, 1956, photo: John Workman

## Richard Mabey

pp. 180/181. View of damage to the trees caused by the storm in October 1987, Sheffield Park, East Sussex, courtesy of The National Trust Photographic Library

p. 182. Norbury Park, photo: Vicki Berger, 1994

p. 183. *The Scrubs*, Norbury Park, photo: Derek Francis, 1995

p. 184. The garden south of the house at Erddig, Clwyd, photo: Rupert Truman, courtesy of National Trust Photographic Library

p. 186. *Trees and Storm Clouds*, Updown Wood, Norbury Park, photo: Derek Francis, 1995

p. 187. Luton Hoo, Bedfordshire, photo: Gillian Darley

p. 189. View showing damage to the trees caused by the storm in October 1987, Sheffield Park, East Sussex, photo: Patsy Fagan, courtesy of the National Trust Photographic Library

p. 190. View showing the damage to the trees in the parkland caused by the storm in October 1987, Wakehurst Place, West Sussex, photo: Mark Marques, courtesy of The National Trust Photographic Library

p. 191. *Towards the Junipers*, Norbury Park, photo: Derek Francis, 1995

p. 192. *Fallen Tree*, Norbury Park, photo: Derek Francis, 1995

# Biographies

**Jay Appleton** is Emeritus Professor of the University of Hull where he taught Geography from 1950 to 1985, holding short visiting appointments at universities in Australia, New Zealand, Canada and the USA. His publications include *The Experience of Landscape, The Symbolism of Habitat* and an autobiographical study, *How I Made the World*. He is a Fellow of the Royal Geographical Society and of the Royal Society of Arts, an Honorary Associate of the Landscape Institute and a past Chair and Honorary Life Member of the Landscape Research Group.

**Vicki Berger** is an architect in private practice who, since 1986, has been focusing on landscape and garden design. She has worked closely with artists and public art administrators on projects such as *The British Rail Time Garden* at Gateshead Garden Festival in 1990 and *the Furnished Landscape* exhibition at the Crafts Council in 1992. In July 1994 she was appointed, with Isabel Vasseur, as joint co-ordinator for South East Arts/Surrey County Council Art and Landscape Project in Norbury Park.

**John Burnside** has published six books of poetry, of which the most recent are *Swimming in the Flood*, and *A Normal Skin* . His first novel *The Dumb House* appeared earlier this year, and he is now working on a new collection of poetry and a second novel. He lives in Fife, within sight of the Firth of Forth, and is Writer in Residence at the University of Dundee.

**Gillian Darley** has been Director of The Landscape Foundation since 1984. From 1990 to 1993 she was the Architecture Correspondent for *The Observer*. She is currently writing a biography of Sir John Soane.

**Richard Hoggart** is founder of the Birmingham Centre for Contemporary Cultural Studies. For five years he was Assistant Director-General at UNESCO at its headquarters in Paris. He was also Warden of Goldsmiths' College, University of London. In 1971 he was the BBC Reith Lecturer. His many publications include *The Uses of Literacy*, two volumes of collected essays *Speaking to Each Other*, *Townscape with Figures: Portrait of an English Town* and *The Way We Live Now*.

**Jane Howarth** studied Philosophy at University College, London; Somerville College, Oxford, and Birmingham University. She is currently a lecturer in Philosophy at the University of Lancaster. Her research focuses on investigating, in the light of environmental problems, the relations between humans and the natural world including the aesthetic appreciation of nature. Her publications include articles on "Nature's Mood", "Beauty in Ruins", "The Crisis of Ecology" and "Ecology: Modern Hero or Postmodern Villain". She is also the co-author of *Understanding Phenomenology*.

**Tania Kovats** won the Barclays Young Artist Award in 1991, shortly after gaining an MA at the Royal College of Art. She has exhibited in mixed exhibitions internationally. Her first solo exhibition was at the Riverside Studios in London with subsequent exhibitions at Lokaal 01 in Breda, Holland, Galleria Rizzo, Paris, and the Statengalerie, Holland. She has also had two solo exhibitions at the Laure Genillard Gallery in London. In 1996 she was awarded the Royal Society of Arts "Art for Architecture Award" for her work in connection with the Ikon Gallery in Birmingham.

**Richard Mabey** has been a freelance writer and broadcaster since 1973. He is currently a Director of Common Ground, a member of the Advisory Board of Plantlife and a member of the Advisory Council of the Open Spaces Society. He won the Whitbread biography award for his book *Gilbert White*. Since 1981 he has owned Hardings Wood in the Chilterns which is run as a community wood. His broadcasting has included *Back to the Roots* (an eight part series), *Tomorrow's World*, and recently *Postcards from the Country*. His publications include *The Oxford Book of Nature Writing*, *Food for Free*, *The Common Ground*  and *Flora Britannica*.

**Eileen O'Keefe** is Senior Lecturer in Philosophy and Health Policy at the University of North London. Her publications include *Divided London: Toward a European Public Health Approach* (with Jenny Newbury) and *Community Health* (with Roger Ottewill and Ann Wall). Recent articles are devoted to World Bank Health Policy and UK compliance with the UN Convention on the Rights of the Child. Current research considers the involvement of housebound service users in public planning. She has also visited the Ukraine where she has been working on a British Council Project. Many of her activities focus on the World Health Organisation's Healthy Cities Project.

**Isabel Vasseur** is Director of Art Project Management, a consultancy service for development agencies, local authorities and the private sector, which she set up to offer advice on Public Art strategy and commissions management. From 1980 to 1986 she pioneered the Public Art movement as agent for Eastern Arts and as an advisor to the Arts Council's 'Works of Art in Public Places' funding scheme. From 1986 to 1990 she was visual arts co-ordinator for both the *Glasgow Garden Festival* and the *National Garden Festival* in Gateshead, while two years later she initiated, organised, and curated *Lux Europae* in Edinburgh, a city-wide exhibition of light installations by international artists to coincide with the European Summit. In July 1994 she was appointed, with Vicki Berger, as joint co-ordinator for South East Arts/Surrey County Council Art and Landscape Project in Norbury Park.

**Richard Wentworth** taught in the School of Art at Goldsmith's College, University of London, from 1971 to 1987. He won the Mark Rothko Memorial Award in 1974 and was a DAAD Fellow in Berlin between 1992 and 1994. He was included in *The British Art Show* in 1984 and subsequently participated in mixed exhibitions internationally. Since 1984 he has had four solo exhibitions at the Lisson Gallery, London, and solo shows at Sala Parpallo, Valencia; the Kohji Ogura Gallery, Nagoya, Japan; Gallerie d'Art Contemporain, Geneva; Museum het Kruithuis, Hertogenbosch, Holland; and Musée des Beaux Arts, Calais. Amongst the catalogues for his exhibitions is *Richard Wentworth* by Marina Warner, published in 1994 following his solo exhibition at the Serpentine Gallery in London. His work is in public and private collections in England and abroad, including the Tate Gallery, London. He currently teaches at The Architectural Association, London.

**John Workman** has been an advisor on conservation and forestry to the National Trust in England, Wales and Northern Ireland since 1950. During the 1960s and 70s he prepared plans for the rejuvenation of some eighty National Trust Landscape Parks, including Petworth, Blickling, Stowe, Stourhead and Boxhill. He developed policies for Woodlands Landscape Conservation and Access and for the long-term treatment of avenues. He is a past President of The Royal Forestry Society, Chair of the Tree Council, a former member of NCC Committee for England, and was on the Exmoor National Park Committee. Presently, he is Chair of the Cotswold Area of Outstanding National Beauty, Chair of the Trustees of Friends of Westonbirt Arboretum, and involved in the management of Family Beechwoods' Sites of Special Scientific Interest and National Nature Reserves and with Gloucestershire Wildlife Trust.

**Ken Worpole** is a researcher, writer, policy advisor, and Senior Associate of Comedia. He has lectured on aspects of literature and urban and cultural policy in the UK, Sweden, France, Italy and Australia. In June 1996 he was awarded a Fellowship by the Foundation for Urban & Regional Studies. His publications include *City Centres, City Cultures* (with Mark Fisher MP), *Towns for People: New Issues in Urban Policy*, *Libraries in a World of Cultural Change* (with Liz Greenhalgh) and *Park Life*, a Comedia/Demos report. He is currently writing a book on the twentieth-century European architecture of public buildings and landscapes.

# Further Reading

Abrioux, Yves, *Ian Hamilton Finlay: A Visual Primer*, London: Reaktion Books, 1992.

Appleton, Jay, *The Experience of Landscape*, New York: John Wiley & Sons, 1975. Revised and expanded second edition, 1992.

Appleton, Jay, *The Symbolism of Habitat: An Interpretation of Landscape in the Arts*, Seattle: University of Washington Press, 1990.

Barrow, John, *The Artful Universe*, Oxford: Oxford University Press, 1995.

Beardsley, John, *Earthworks and Beyond: Contemporary Art in the Landscape*, New York: Abbeville Press, 1989.

Clough, Wilson O., *The Necessary Earth*, Austin: University of Texas Press, 1964.

Daniels, Stephen, *Fields of Vision: Landscape Imagery and National Identity in England and the United States*, Oxford: Polity Press with Blackwell Publishers, 1993.

Daniels, Stephen & Charles Watkins, *The Picturesque Landscape. Visions of Georgian Herefordshire*, Nottingham: Department of Geography, University of Nottingham, 1994.

Davis, Peter & Tony Knipe, *A Sense of Place: Sculpture in Landscape*, Sunderland: Coelfrith Press/Sunderland Arts Centre, 1984

Descombes, Georges, et al., *Voie suisse. L'itinéraire genevois. De Morschach à Brunnen*, République et Canton de Genève, 1991.

De Ville, Nicholas & Stephen Foster, *Space Invaders: Issues of Representation, Context and Meaning in Contemporary Art*, Southampton: John Hansard Gallery, 1993.

Hunt, John Dixon & Peter Willis, *The Genius of the Place. The English Landscape Garden 1620-1820*, Cambridge Massachusetts: The MIT Press, 1988.

Everett, Nigel, *The Tory View of Landscape*, New Haven Connecticut: Yale University Press, 1994.

Fieldhouse, Ken, & Sheila Harvey, *Landscape Design—An International Survey*, London: Laurence King Publishing, 1992.

Grant, Bill & Paul Harris, *The Grizedale Experience: Sculpture, Arts and Theatre in a Lakeland Forest*, Edinburgh: Canongate Press, 1991.

Greenhalgh, Liz & Ken Worpole, *Park Life: Urban Parks and Social Renewal*, London: Comedia/Demos, 1995.

Hunt, John Dixon, *Bernard Lassus in Eden*, Milan: Automobilia, 1995.

Hussey, Christopher, *The Picturesque: Studies in a Point of View*, London: Putnam, 1927.

Kaplan, Stephen & Rachel, *The Experience of Nature: A Psychological Perspective*, Cambridge: Cambridge University Press, 1989.

Kemal, Salem & Ivan Gaskell, *Landscape, Natural Beauty and the Arts*, Cambridge: Cambridge University Press, 1993.

Linardo, Mark, *Car, Culture and the Countryside Change*, London: National Trust, 1996.

Murray, Graeme, ed., *Art in the Garden* Glasgow Garden Festival, Edinburgh: Graeme Murray, 1988.

Nash, David, *Forms into Time*, London: Academy Group, 1996.

Schama, Simon, *Landscape and Memory*, New York: Harper Collins, 1995.

Selwood, Sara, *The Benefits of Public Art: The Polemics of Permanent Art in Public Places*, London: Policy Studies Institute, 1995.

Shepheard, Paul, *The Cultivated Wilderness or What is Landscape?*, Cambridge Massachusetts: The MIT Press, 1997.

Spens, Michael, *Gardens of the Mind: The Genius of Geoffrey Jellicoe*, Suffolk: Antique Collectors Club, 1992.

Stroud, Dorothy, *Humphry Repton*, London: Country Life, 1962.

Stroud, Dorothy, *Capability Brown*, London: Faber, 1975.

Wrede, Stuart & William Howard Adams, *Denatured Visions. Landscape & Culture in the Twentieth Century*, New York: Museum of Modern Art, 1991.

Taylor, Hilary, *Age and Order: The Public Park as a Metaphor for Civilised Society*, London: Comedia Working Paper, 1995.

Zagari, Franco, L'Architectura del Giardino Contemporaneo, Milan: Arnoldo Mondadori Editore/Rome: De Luca Edizioni d'Arte Spa, 1988.

Crabtree, Amanda, ed., *Public Art*, London: Academy Group, 1996.

*Leisure Landscapes: Leisure, Culture & the English Countryside: Challenges and Conflicts*, London: Council for the Protection of Rural England, 1994.

*Landscape Architecture Europe*, Reigate: Landscape Design Trust, 1994.

# Colophon

Originated and edited by
Vicki Berger and Isabel Vasseur
Texts edited by Victoria Walsh
Picture Research by Dee Robinson
and Vicki Berger
Designed by Maria Beddoes and Paul Khera
assisted by Mark Hutchinson
Produced by Duncan McCorquodale

Printed by PJ Reproductions in the
European Union
© 1997 Black Dog Publishing Limited,
authors and artists.
British Library Cataloging-in-Publication Data.
A catalogue record for this book is available from
The British Library.

Library of Congress Cataloging-in-Publication Data:
*Arcadia Revisted. The Place of Landscape.*

ISBN 1 901 033 70 8

Cover
Tania Kovats, *Canyon*
Back cover
Tania Kovats, *Gortex*

# Acknowledgements

Vicki Berger and Isabel Vasseur would like to thank the authors for their contributions to this publication and for advancing the debate on the state and future of the landscape and its management. Thanks are also due to the Arts Council of England, South East Arts and Surrey County Council for funding the Norbury Park Art and Landscape Project, the subsequent symposium 'Arcadia Revisited' and this publication. Thanks also go to the following individuals: Jane Heath, Philip Bintcliffe, Andrew Brighton (Tate Gallery), Catherine Brighton, Caroline Collier (previously Visual Arts & Crafts Manager, SEA), Teresa Gleadowe (Royal College of Art), Lisa Creaye-Griffin, Claire Holloway, Imogen Haig, Alan Oakley and Graham Manning of Surrey County Council, Dee Robinson, Jeremy Theophilus and Peter Greig of the Arts Council of England, Jim Shea of South East Arts, Michaela Crimmin of the Royal Society of Arts, Grace Sharp and Roman Vasseur of Art Project Management, Victoria Walsh, and finally Duncan McCorquodale.